Mometrix
TEST PREPARATION

I0878913

TOEFL

Essentials®
Secrets Study Guide

DEAR FUTURE EXAM SUCCESS STORY

First of all, **THANK YOU** for purchasing Mometrix study materials!

Second, congratulations! You are one of the few determined test-takers who are committed to doing whatever it takes to excel on your exam. **You have come to the right place.** We developed these study materials with one goal in mind: to deliver you the information you need in a format that's concise and easy to use.

In addition to optimizing your guide for the content of the test, we've outlined our recommended steps for breaking down the preparation process into small, attainable goals so you can make sure you stay on track.

We've also analyzed the entire test-taking process, identifying the most common pitfalls and showing how you can overcome them and be ready for any curveball the test throws you.

Standardized testing is one of the biggest obstacles on your road to success, which only increases the importance of doing well in the high-pressure, high-stakes environment of test day. Your results on this test could have a significant impact on your future, and this guide provides the information and practical advice to help you achieve your full potential on test day.

Your success is our success

We would love to hear from you! If you would like to share the story of your exam success or if you have any questions or comments in regard to our products, please contact us at **800-673-8175** or **support@mometrix.com**.

Thanks again for your business and we wish you continued success!

Sincerely,
The Mometrix Test Preparation Team

Need more help? Check out our flashcards at:
http://MometrixFlashcards.com/TOEFL

Table of Contents

Introduction

Thank you for purchasing this resource! You have made the choice to prepare yourself for a test that could have a huge impact on your future, and this guide is designed to help you be fully ready for test day. Obviously, it's important to have a solid understanding of the test material, but you also need to be prepared for the unique environment and stressors of the test, so that you can perform to the best of your abilities.

For this purpose, the first section that appears in this guide is the **Secret Keys**. We've devoted countless hours to meticulously researching what works and what doesn't, and we've boiled down our findings to the five most impactful steps you can take to improve your performance on the test. We start at the beginning with study planning and move through the preparation process, all the way to the testing strategies that will help you get the most out of what you know when you're finally sitting in front of the test.

We recommend that you start preparing for your test as far in advance as possible. However, if you've bought this guide as a last-minute study resource and only have a few days before your test, we recommend that you skip over the first two Secret Keys since they address a long-term study plan.

If you struggle with **test anxiety**, we strongly encourage you to check out our recommendations for how you can overcome it. Test anxiety is a formidable foe, but it can be beaten, and we want to make sure you have the tools you need to defeat it.

Secret Key #1 – Plan Big, Study Small

There's a lot riding on your performance. If you want to ace this test, you're going to need to keep your skills sharp and the material fresh in your mind. You need a plan that lets you review everything you need to know while still fitting in your schedule. We'll break this strategy down into three categories.

Information Organization

Start with the information you already have: the official test outline. From this, you can make a complete list of all the concepts you need to cover before the test. Organize these concepts into groups that can be studied together, and create a list of any related vocabulary you need to learn so you can brush up on any difficult terms. You'll want to keep this vocabulary list handy once you actually start studying since you may need to add to it along the way.

Time Management

Once you have your set of study concepts, decide how to spread them out over the time you have left before the test. Break your study plan into small, clear goals so you have a manageable task for each day and know exactly what you're doing. Then just focus on one small step at a time. When you manage your time this way, you don't need to spend hours at a time studying. Studying a small block of content for a short period each day helps you retain information better and avoid stressing over how much you have left to do. You can relax knowing that you have a plan to cover everything in time. In order for this strategy to be effective though, you have to start studying early and stick to your schedule. Avoid the exhaustion and futility that comes from last-minute cramming!

Study Environment

The environment you study in has a big impact on your learning. Studying in a coffee shop, while probably more enjoyable, is not likely to be as fruitful as studying in a quiet room. It's important to keep distractions to a minimum. You're only planning to study for a short block of time, so make the most of it. Don't pause to check your phone or get up to find a snack. It's also important to **avoid multitasking**. Research has consistently shown that multitasking will make your studying dramatically less effective. Your study area should also be comfortable and well-lit so you don't have the distraction of straining your eyes or sitting on an uncomfortable chair.

The time of day you study is also important. You want to be rested and alert. Don't wait until just before bedtime. Study when you'll be most likely to comprehend and remember. Even better, if you know what time of day your test will be, set that time aside for study. That way your brain will be used to working on that subject at that specific time and you'll have a better chance of recalling information.

Finally, it can be helpful to team up with others who are studying for the same test. Your actual studying should be done in as isolated an environment as possible, but the work of organizing the information and setting up the study plan can be divided up. In between study sessions, you can discuss with your teammates the concepts that you're all studying and quiz each other on the details. Just be sure that your teammates are as serious about the test as you are. If you find that your study time is being replaced with social time, you might need to find a new team.

Secret Key #2 – Make Your Studying Count

You're devoting a lot of time and effort to preparing for this test, so you want to be absolutely certain it will pay off. This means doing more than just reading the content and hoping you can remember it on test day. It's important to make every minute of study count. There are two main areas you can focus on to make your studying count.

Retention

It doesn't matter how much time you study if you can't remember the material. You need to make sure you are retaining the concepts. To check your retention of the information you're learning, try recalling it at later times with minimal prompting. Try carrying around flashcards and glance at one or two from time to time or ask a friend who's also studying for the test to quiz you.

To enhance your retention, look for ways to put the information into practice so that you can apply it rather than simply recalling it. If you're using the information in practical ways, it will be much easier to remember. Similarly, it helps to solidify a concept in your mind if you're not only reading it to yourself but also explaining it to someone else. Ask a friend to let you teach them about a concept you're a little shaky on (or speak aloud to an imaginary audience if necessary). As you try to summarize, define, give examples, and answer your friend's questions, you'll understand the concepts better and they will stay with you longer. Finally, step back for a big picture view and ask yourself how each piece of information fits with the whole subject. When you link the different concepts together and see them working together as a whole, it's easier to remember the individual components.

Finally, practice showing your work on any multi-step problems, even if you're just studying. Writing out each step you take to solve a problem will help solidify the process in your mind, and you'll be more likely to remember it during the test.

Modality

Modality simply refers to the means or method by which you study. Choosing a study modality that fits your own individual learning style is crucial. No two people learn best in exactly the same way, so it's important to know your strengths and use them to your advantage.

For example, if you learn best by visualization, focus on visualizing a concept in your mind and draw an image or a diagram. Try color-coding your notes, illustrating them, or creating symbols that will trigger your mind to recall a learned concept. If you learn best by hearing or discussing information, find a study partner who learns the same way or read aloud to yourself. Think about how to put the information in your own words. Imagine that you are giving a lecture on the topic and record yourself so you can listen to it later.

For any learning style, flashcards can be helpful. Organize the information so you can take advantage of spare moments to review. Underline key words or phrases. Use different colors for different categories. Mnemonic devices (such as creating a short list in which every item starts with the same letter) can also help with retention. Find what works best for you and use it to store the information in your mind most effectively and easily.

Secret Key #3 – Practice the Right Way

Your success on test day depends not only on how many hours you put into preparing, but also on whether you prepared the right way. It's good to check along the way to see if your studying is paying off. One of the most effective ways to do this is by taking practice tests to evaluate your progress. Practice tests are useful because they show exactly where you need to improve. Every time you take a practice test, pay special attention to these three groups of questions:

- The questions you got wrong
- The questions you had to guess on, even if you guessed right
- The questions you found difficult or slow to work through

This will show you exactly what your weak areas are, and where you need to devote more study time. Ask yourself why each of these questions gave you trouble. Was it because you didn't understand the material? Was it because you didn't remember the vocabulary? Do you need more repetitions on this type of question to build speed and confidence? Dig into those questions and figure out how you can strengthen your weak areas as you go back to review the material.

Additionally, many practice tests have a section explaining the answer choices. It can be tempting to read the explanation and think that you now have a good understanding of the concept. However, an explanation likely only covers part of the question's broader context. Even if the explanation makes perfect sense, **go back and investigate** every concept related to the question until you're positive you have a thorough understanding.

As you go along, keep in mind that the practice test is just that: practice. Memorizing these questions and answers will not be very helpful on the actual test because it is unlikely to have any of the same exact questions. If you only know the right answers to the sample questions, you won't be prepared for the real thing. **Study the concepts** until you understand them fully, and then you'll be able to answer any question that shows up on the test.

It's important to wait on the practice tests until you're ready. If you take a test on your first day of study, you may be overwhelmed by the amount of material covered and how much you need to learn. Work up to it gradually.

On test day, you'll need to be prepared for answering questions, managing your time, and using the test-taking strategies you've learned. It's a lot to balance, like a mental marathon that will have a big impact on your future. Like training for a marathon, you'll need to start slowly and work your way up. When test day arrives, you'll be ready.

Start with the strategies you've read in the first two Secret Keys—plan your course and study in the way that works best for you. If you have time, consider using multiple study resources to get different approaches to the same concepts. It can be helpful to see difficult concepts from more than one angle. Then find a good source for practice tests. Many times, the test website will suggest potential study resources or provide sample tests.

Practice Test Strategy

If you're able to find at least three practice tests, we recommend this strategy:

Untimed and Open-Book Practice

Take the first test with no time constraints and with your notes and study guide handy. Take your time and focus on applying the strategies you've learned.

Timed and Open-Book Practice

Take the second practice test open-book as well, but set a timer and practice pacing yourself to finish in time.

Timed and Closed-Book Practice

Take any other practice tests as if it were test day. Set a timer and put away your study materials. Sit at a table or desk in a quiet room, imagine yourself at the testing center, and answer questions as quickly and accurately as possible.

Keep repeating timed and closed-book tests on a regular basis until you run out of practice tests or it's time for the actual test. Your mind will be ready for the schedule and stress of test day, and you'll be able to focus on recalling the material you've learned.

Secret Key #4 – Pace Yourself

Once you're fully prepared for the material on the test, your biggest challenge on test day will be managing your time. Just knowing that the clock is ticking can make you panic even if you have plenty of time left. Work on pacing yourself so you can build confidence against the time constraints of the exam. Pacing is a difficult skill to master, especially in a high-pressure environment, so **practice is vital**.

Set time expectations for your pace based on how much time is available. For example, if a section has 60 questions and the time limit is 30 minutes, you know you have to average 30 seconds or less per question in order to answer them all. Although 30 seconds is the hard limit, set 25 seconds per question as your goal, so you reserve extra time to spend on harder questions. When you budget extra time for the harder questions, you no longer have any reason to stress when those questions take longer to answer.

Don't let this time expectation distract you from working through the test at a calm, steady pace, but keep it in mind so you don't spend too much time on any one question. Recognize that taking extra time on one question you don't understand may keep you from answering two that you do understand later in the test. If your time limit for a question is up and you're still not sure of the answer, mark it and move on, and come back to it later if the time and the test format allow. If the testing format doesn't allow you to return to earlier questions, just make an educated guess; then put it out of your mind and move on.

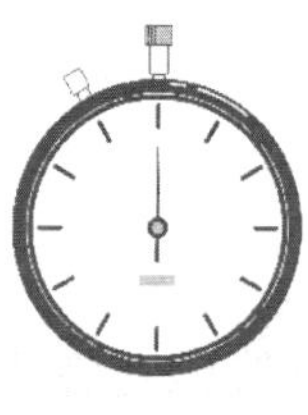

On the easier questions, be careful not to rush. It may seem wise to hurry through them so you have more time for the challenging ones, but it's not worth missing one if you know the concept and just didn't take the time to read the question fully. Work efficiently but make sure you understand the question and have looked at all of the answer choices, since more than one may seem right at first.

Even if you're paying attention to the time, you may find yourself a little behind at some point. You should speed up to get back on track, but do so wisely. Don't panic; just take a few seconds less on each question until you're caught up. Don't guess without thinking, but do look through the answer choices and eliminate any you know are wrong. If you can get down to two choices, it is often worthwhile to guess from those. Once you've chosen an answer, move on and don't dwell on any that you skipped or had to hurry through. If a question was taking too long, chances are it was one of the harder ones, so you weren't as likely to get it right anyway.

On the other hand, if you find yourself getting ahead of schedule, it may be beneficial to slow down a little. The more quickly you work, the more likely you are to make a careless mistake that will affect your score. You've budgeted time for each question, so don't be afraid to spend that time. Practice an efficient but careful pace to get the most out of the time you have.

Secret Key #5 – Have a Plan for Guessing

When you're taking the test, you may find yourself stuck on a question. Some of the answer choices seem better than others, but you don't see the one answer choice that is obviously correct. What do you do?

The scenario described above is very common, yet most test takers have not effectively prepared for it. Developing and practicing a plan for guessing may be one of the single most effective uses of your time as you get ready for the exam.

In developing your plan for guessing, there are three questions to address:

- When should you start the guessing process?
- How should you narrow down the choices?
- Which answer should you choose?

When to Start the Guessing Process

Unless your plan for guessing is to select C every time (which, despite its merits, is not what we recommend), you need to leave yourself enough time to apply your answer elimination strategies. Since you have a limited amount of time for each question, that means that if you're going to give yourself the best shot at guessing correctly, you have to decide quickly whether or not you will guess.

Of course, the best-case scenario is that you don't have to guess at all, so first, see if you can answer the question based on your knowledge of the subject and basic reasoning skills. Focus on the key words in the question and try to jog your memory of related topics. Give yourself a chance to bring the knowledge to mind, but once you realize that you don't have (or you can't access) the knowledge you need to answer the question, it's time to start the guessing process.

It's almost always better to start the guessing process too early than too late. It only takes a few seconds to remember something and answer the question from knowledge. Carefully eliminating wrong answer choices takes longer. Plus, going through the process of eliminating answer choices can actually help jog your memory.

Summary: Start the guessing process as soon as you decide that you can't answer the question based on your knowledge.

How to Narrow Down the Choices

The next chapter in this book (**Test-Taking Strategies**) includes a wide range of strategies for how to approach questions and how to look for answer choices to eliminate. You will definitely want to read those carefully, practice them, and figure out which ones work best for you. Here though, we're going to address a mindset rather than a particular strategy.

Your odds of guessing an answer correctly depend on how many options you are choosing from.

Number of options left	5	4	3	2	1
Odds of guessing correctly	20%	25%	33%	50%	100%

You can see from this chart just how valuable it is to be able to eliminate incorrect answers and make an educated guess, but there are two things that many test takers do that cause them to miss out on the benefits of guessing:

- Accidentally eliminating the correct answer
- Selecting an answer based on an impression

We'll look at the first one here, and the second one in the next section.

To avoid accidentally eliminating the correct answer, we recommend a thought exercise called **the $5 challenge**. In this challenge, you only eliminate an answer choice from contention if you are willing to bet $5 on it being wrong. Why $5? Five dollars is a small but not insignificant amount of money. It's an amount you could afford to lose but wouldn't want to throw away. And while losing $5 once might not hurt too much, doing it twenty times will set you back $100. In the same way, each small decision you make—eliminating a choice here, guessing on a question there—won't by itself impact your score very much, but when you put them all together, they can make a big difference. By holding each answer choice elimination decision to a higher standard, you can reduce the risk of accidentally eliminating the correct answer.

The $5 challenge can also be applied in a positive sense: If you are willing to bet $5 that an answer choice *is* correct, go ahead and mark it as correct.

Summary: Only eliminate an answer choice if you are willing to bet $5 that it is wrong.

Which Answer to Choose

You're taking the test. You've run into a hard question and decided you'll have to guess. You've eliminated all the answer choices you're willing to bet $5 on. Now you have to pick an answer. Why do we even need to talk about this? Why can't you just pick whichever one you feel like when the time comes?

The answer to these questions is that if you don't come into the test with a plan, you'll rely on your impression to select an answer choice, and if you do that, you risk falling into a trap. The test writers know that everyone who takes their test will be guessing on some of the questions, so they intentionally write wrong answer choices to seem plausible. You still have to pick an answer though, and if the wrong answer choices are designed to look right, how can you ever be sure that you're not falling for their trap? The best solution we've found to this dilemma is to take the decision out of your hands entirely. Here is the process we recommend:

Once you've eliminated any choices that you are confident (willing to bet $5) are wrong, select the first remaining choice as your answer.

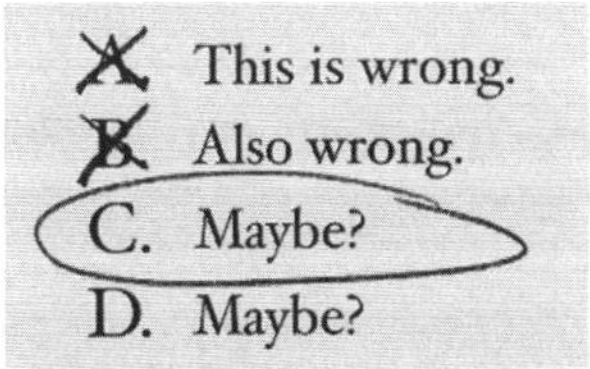

Whether you choose to select the first remaining choice, the second, or the last, the important thing is that you use some preselected standard. Using this approach guarantees that you will not be enticed into selecting an answer choice that looks right, because you are not basing your decision on how the answer choices look.

This is not meant to make you question your knowledge. Instead, it is to help you recognize the difference between your knowledge and your impressions. There's a huge difference between thinking an answer is right because of what you know, and thinking an answer is right because it looks or sounds like it should be right.

Summary: To ensure that your selection is appropriately random, make a predetermined selection from among all answer choices you have not eliminated.

Test-Taking Strategies

This section contains a list of test-taking strategies that you may find helpful as you work through the test. By taking what you know and applying logical thought, you can maximize your chances of answering any question correctly!

It is very important to realize that every question is different and every person is different: no single strategy will work on every question, and no single strategy will work for every person. That's why we've included all of them here, so you can try them out and determine which ones work best for different types of questions and which ones work best for you.

Question Strategies

⊘ Read Carefully

Read the question and the answer choices carefully. Don't miss the question because you misread the terms. You have plenty of time to read each question thoroughly and make sure you understand what is being asked. Yet a happy medium must be attained, so don't waste too much time. You must read carefully and efficiently.

⊘ Contextual Clues

Look for contextual clues. If the question includes a word you are not familiar with, look at the immediate context for some indication of what the word might mean. Contextual clues can often give you all the information you need to decipher the meaning of an unfamiliar word. Even if you can't determine the meaning, you may be able to narrow down the possibilities enough to make a solid guess at the answer to the question.

⊘ Prefixes

If you're having trouble with a word in the question or answer choices, try dissecting it. Take advantage of every clue that the word might include. Prefixes can be a huge help. Usually, they allow you to determine a basic meaning. *Pre-* means before, *post-* means after, *pro-* is positive, *de-* is negative. From prefixes, you can get an idea of the general meaning of the word and try to put it into context.

⊘ Hedge Words

Watch out for critical hedge words, such as *likely, may, can, often, almost, mostly, usually, generally, rarely,* and *sometimes*. Question writers insert these hedge phrases to cover every possibility. Often an answer choice will be wrong simply because it leaves no room for exception. Be on guard for answer choices that have definitive words such as *exactly* and *always*.

⊘ Switchback Words

Stay alert for *switchbacks*. These are the words and phrases frequently used to alert you to shifts in thought. The most common switchback words are *but, although*, and *however*. Others include *nevertheless, on the other hand, even though, while, in spite of, despite*, and *regardless of*. Switchback words are important to catch because they can change the direction of the question or an answer choice.

⊘ FACE VALUE

When in doubt, use common sense. Accept the situation in the problem at face value. Don't read too much into it. These problems will not require you to make wild assumptions. If you have to go beyond creativity and warp time or space in order to have an answer choice fit the question, then you should move on and consider the other answer choices. These are normal problems rooted in reality. The applicable relationship or explanation may not be readily apparent, but it is there for you to figure out. Use your common sense to interpret anything that isn't clear.

Answer Choice Strategies

⊘ ANSWER SELECTION

The most thorough way to pick an answer choice is to identify and eliminate wrong answers until only one is left, then confirm it is the correct answer. Sometimes an answer choice may immediately seem right, but be careful. The test writers will usually put more than one reasonable answer choice on each question, so take a second to read all of them and make sure that the other choices are not equally obvious. As long as you have time left, it is better to read every answer choice than to pick the first one that looks right without checking the others.

⊘ ANSWER CHOICE FAMILIES

An answer choice family consists of two (in rare cases, three) answer choices that are very similar in construction and cannot all be true at the same time. If you see two answer choices that are direct opposites or parallels, one of them is usually the correct answer. For instance, if one answer choice says that quantity *x* increases and another either says that quantity *x* decreases (opposite) or says that quantity *y* increases (parallel), then those answer choices would fall into the same family. An answer choice that doesn't match the construction of the answer choice family is more likely to be incorrect. Most questions will not have answer choice families, but when they do appear, you should be prepared to recognize them.

⊘ ELIMINATE ANSWERS

Eliminate answer choices as soon as you realize they are wrong, but make sure you consider all possibilities. If you are eliminating answer choices and realize that the last one you are left with is also wrong, don't panic. Start over and consider each choice again. There may be something you missed the first time that you will realize on the second pass.

⊘ AVOID FACT TRAPS

Don't be distracted by an answer choice that is factually true but doesn't answer the question. You are looking for the choice that answers the question. Stay focused on what the question is asking for so you don't accidentally pick an answer that is true but incorrect. Always go back to the question and make sure the answer choice you've selected actually answers the question and is not merely a true statement.

⊘ EXTREME STATEMENTS

In general, you should avoid answers that put forth extreme actions as standard practice or proclaim controversial ideas as established fact. An answer choice that states the "process should be used in certain situations, if..." is much more likely to be correct than one that states the "process should be discontinued completely." The first is a calm rational statement and doesn't even make a definitive, uncompromising stance, using a hedge word *if* to provide wiggle room, whereas the second choice is far more extreme.

⊘ BENCHMARK

As you read through the answer choices and you come across one that seems to answer the question well, mentally select that answer choice. This is not your final answer, but it's the one that will help you evaluate the other answer choices. The one that you selected is your benchmark or standard for judging each of the other answer choices. Every other answer choice must be compared to your benchmark. That choice is correct until proven otherwise by another answer choice beating it. If you find a better answer, then that one becomes your new benchmark. Once you've decided that no other choice answers the question as well as your benchmark, you have your final answer.

⊘ PREDICT THE ANSWER

Before you even start looking at the answer choices, it is often best to try to predict the answer. When you come up with the answer on your own, it is easier to avoid distractions and traps because you will know exactly what to look for. The right answer choice is unlikely to be word-for-word what you came up with, but it should be a close match. Even if you are confident that you have the right answer, you should still take the time to read each option before moving on.

General Strategies

⊘ TOUGH QUESTIONS

If you are stumped on a problem or it appears too hard or too difficult, don't waste time. Move on! Remember though, if you can quickly check for obviously incorrect answer choices, your chances of guessing correctly are greatly improved. Before you completely give up, at least try to knock out a couple of possible answers. Eliminate what you can and then guess at the remaining answer choices before moving on.

⊘ CHECK YOUR WORK

Since you will probably not know every term listed and the answer to every question, it is important that you get credit for the ones that you do know. Don't miss any questions through careless mistakes. If at all possible, try to take a second to look back over your answer selection and make sure you've selected the correct answer choice and haven't made a costly careless mistake (such as marking an answer choice that you didn't mean to mark). This quick double check should more than pay for itself in caught mistakes for the time it costs.

⊘ PACE YOURSELF

It's easy to be overwhelmed when you're looking at a page full of questions; your mind is confused and full of random thoughts, and the clock is ticking down faster than you would like. Calm down and maintain the pace that you have set for yourself. Especially as you get down to the last few minutes of the test, don't let the small numbers on the clock make you panic. As long as you are on track by monitoring your pace, you are guaranteed to have time for each question.

⊘ DON'T RUSH

It is very easy to make errors when you are in a hurry. Maintaining a fast pace in answering questions is pointless if it makes you miss questions that you would have gotten right otherwise. Test writers like to include distracting information and wrong answers that seem right. Taking a little extra time to avoid careless mistakes can make all the difference in your test score. Find a pace that allows you to be confident in the answers that you select.

⊘ KEEP MOVING

Panicking will not help you pass the test, so do your best to stay calm and keep moving. Taking deep breaths and going through the answer elimination steps you practiced can help to break through a stress barrier and keep your pace.

Final Notes

The combination of a solid foundation of content knowledge and the confidence that comes from practicing your plan for applying that knowledge is the key to maximizing your performance on test day. As your foundation of content knowledge is built up and strengthened, you'll find that the strategies included in this chapter become more and more effective in helping you quickly sift through the distractions and traps of the test to isolate the correct answer.

Now that you're preparing to move forward into the test content chapters of this book, be sure to keep your goal in mind. As you read, think about how you will be able to apply this information on the test. If you've already seen sample questions for the test and you have an idea of the question format and style, try to come up with questions of your own that you can answer based on what you're reading. This will give you valuable practice applying your knowledge in the same ways you can expect to on test day.

Good luck and good studying!

Listening

The Listening section of the TOEFL Essentials consists of a total of 30-45 questions and will last between 21 and 34 minutes. There will be four listening tasks, including listen and reply, listen to a conversation, listen to announcements, and listen to academic talks.

The listen and reply questions ask a simple question and require you to select an appropriate response from four choices. For the other questions, you are listening to a short sample in different contexts, followed by a set of questions about each. These samples include conversations, announcements in an academic setting, and a lecture or talk in an academic setting.

Tips for the Listening Section

The listening section requires you to demonstrate your ability to understand verbal information and use pragmatic understanding to interpret content, tone, and purpose.

Tip 1: Listening for Basic Comprehension

When preparing for the test, take some time to find English radio, lectures, podcasts, and videos to watch and listen to. You should pick different types of sources because during this section of the test, you will be exposed to both academic and everyday English. Practice taking mental notes of what is said and try listening for main points.

Tip 2: Listening for Pragmatic Understanding

Speakers use tone and emphasis in speech to create a certain mood or to accomplish a certain goal. After you are comfortable with listening for basic comprehension, try listening for tone and try to identify a speaker's purpose. Try also to identify whether a speaker is talking more casually or informatively and if there is a particular emotion conveyed.

Tip 3: Connecting and Synthesizing Information

As you listen to speakers talk, you will have to connect information to form conclusions. Try to notice if two speakers make opposing points or if there is a reason behind what is said. After you listen to a sample of speech, practice summarizing and restating information, then listen again to check yourself.

Listening Skills

Use the Pictures

The pictures are provided to orient you to the atmosphere and environment in which the speakers are conducting their conversation. Use those pictures as much as possible. Try to put yourself in that environment. Become one of the pictured speakers and you will be able to better appreciate the conversation and what it means.

Use Multiple Inputs

The questions will be read to you at the same time they are exposed on the screen in the form of text. Take advantage of this. Use both the visual and auditory information being presented to better understand what is being asked. Some people are better visual and some better auditory receivers of information. Since both methods of presenting questions are given, use them both to your maximum advantage.

MAIN IDEAS

Important words and main ideas in conversation are ones that will come up again and again. Listen carefully for any word or words that come up repeatedly. What words come up in nearly every statement made? These words with high frequency are likely to be in the main idea of the conversation. For example, in a conversation about class size in the business department of a college, the term "class size" is likely to appear in nearly every statement made by either speaker in the discussion.

VOICE CHANGES

On the TOEFL, you are expected to be able to recognize and interpret nuances of speech. Be on the alert for any changes in voice, which might register surprise, excitement, or another emotion. If a speaker is talking in a normal monotone voice and suddenly raises their voice to a high pitch, that is a huge clue that something critical is being stated. Listen for a speaker to change their voice and understand the meaning of what they are saying.

Example:

Man: Let's go to Wal-mart.

Woman: *There's a Wal-mart in this small town?*

If the woman's statement was higher pitched, indicating surprise and shock, then she probably did not expect there to be a Wal-mart in that town.

Speakers may also place stronger stress on words that are important, which helps in understanding the focal point of a sentence or can even change sentence meaning.

Example:

Man: Did *you* play baseball over the weekend?

Woman: *We* didn't play baseball. We *watched* a baseball game over the weekend.

Example:

Man: Did you play *baseball* over the weekend?

Woman: We didn't play *baseball;* we played *tennis* instead.

In these examples, the subject of the man's question changes based on which word receives the stress.

SPECIFICS

Listen carefully for specific pieces of information. Adjectives are commonly asked about in TOEFL questions. Try to remember any main adjectives that are mentioned. Pick out adjectives such as numbers, colors, or sizes.

Example:

Man: Let's go to the store and get some apples to make the pie.

Woman: How many do we need?

Man: We'll need **five** apples to make the pie.

A typical question might be about how many apples were needed.

Interpret

As you are listening to the conversation, put yourself in the person's shoes. Think about why someone would make a statement. You'll need to do more than just regurgitate the spoken words; you must also interpret them.

Example:

Woman: I think I'm sick with the flu.

Man: Why don't you go see the campus doctor?

Sample Question: Why did the man mention the campus doctor?

Answer: The campus doctor would be able to determine if the woman had the flu.

Find the Hidden Meaning

Look for the meaning behind a statement. When a speaker answers a question with a statement that doesn't immediately seem to answer the question, the response probably contains a hidden meaning that you will need to recognize and explain.

Man: Are you going to be ready for your presentation?

Woman: I've only got half of it finished and it's taken me five hours just to do this much. There's only an hour left before the presentation is due.

At first, the woman did not seem to answer the question the man presented. She responded with a statement that only seemed loosely related. Once you look deeper, then you can find the true meaning of what she said. If it took the woman five hours to do the first half of the presentation, then it would logically take her another five hours to do the second half. Since she only has one hour until her presentation is due, she would probably NOT be ready for the presentation. So, while an answer was not immediately visible to the man's question, when you applied logic to her response, you could find the hidden meaning.

Types of Listening Problems

Types of Conversations on the TOEFL

On your test, you will encounter a variety of listening prompts which may include one or more speakers. These may include more academic or more informal speakers who may either agree or disagree with one another. You must be able to determine main ideas and viewpoints when encountering conversations.

Academic Conversations

Academic conversations are conversations on a college campus between professors, students, and other campus members. You will need to be able to summarize main ideas and recall important details.

Class Discussions

Class discussions are conversations in a classroom between professors and students. You will need to be able to summarize main ideas, but usually NOT need to recall important details.

Academic Talks

Academic talks are conversations in an orientation meeting on academic courses and procedures or where a professor might discuss a variety of college topics. You will need to be able to summarize main ideas, but usually NOT need to recall important details.

Lectures

Lectures are conversations in a classroom about academic topics. You will need to be able to summarize main ideas, and be able to answer questions such as: who, what, when, where, or why?

Active Listening

Although listening appears to be a passive process, it must be **active** in order to be effective. Indeed, the listener should have a **purpose** for listening. The precise purpose of listening need not be conscious in the mind of the listener. In general, there are four distinguished **intentions** of listening: comprehension, criticism, empathy, and appreciation. These intentions are often intermingled in the same act of listening. When we listen for comprehension, we are trying to understand the message the speaker is communicating. In order to listen for comprehension, we need to know the standards of grammar and punctuation in English. We also need to know the common forms of argument. We also need to have an understanding of the context in which the words are spoken so that we can understand the relationship between message and context.

Listening for the Purposes of Criticism

In order to listen for the purposes of criticism, one must usually also be listening for **comprehension**. It is true that in order to accurately assess the quality of a verbal communication, you will need to understand the content of the communication first. To a certain degree, however, we all apply critical listening skills to communication we have yet to fully understand. For instance, when we hear an advertisement on the radio, we know immediately that the speaker is trying to sell us something, and so we are naturally receptive or skeptical of the message, depending on our preexisting interest in the product or service. In this case, our **critical listening skills** are influencing our listening even before we have begun to comprehend the content.

Listening for Content

In almost every listening situation, the audience is required to listen for **information**. A communication can only be considered effective if the message communicates the information intended by the speaker. The **feedback** issued by the audience indicates the degree to which the information has been received accurately. When the audience is required to ask for clarification or repetition of the message, it is possible that the speaker has been ineffective in delivering his or her information. Moreover, if the audience provides no verbal feedback about a delivered message, it is possible that they either do not understand any of the message or are simply not interested in it. Of course, when there is no verbal feedback it is also possible that the audience simply understands the transmitted message perfectly and requires no clarification or elaboration.

Listening for Comprehension

There are five basic kinds of **intentional listening**: appreciative, therapeutic, discriminative, comprehensive, and critical. **Listening for comprehension** is probably the most familiar form of listening. Students in a classroom are engaged in listening for comprehension when they take notes during a lecture. Whenever we listen to an informative or persuasive speech in order to obtain information about a subject, we are engaged in listening for comprehension. The validity and accuracy of other forms of listening, such as critical listening and discriminative listening, depend on effective listening for comprehension. If an individual is unable to understand the message that is being presented, he or she will not be able to critique it insightfully.

Assessing the Characteristics of the Speaker

As part of the overall critique of a speech, an audience member should consider the personal **characteristics of the speaker**. For instance, the audience member might consider what he or she knew about the speaker before the speech, and then decide whether this information had any influence on his or her interpretation of the speaker's message. The audience member might also consider whether the speaker's personal presentation indicated credibility or made his or her message difficult to believe. Many times, a speaker with a good message and solid supporting materials comes across as vague and disorganized because of his or her physical appearance and vocal mannerisms. Audience members should try to distinguish between weaknesses in the speaker's message and weaknesses in the speaker's personal presentation.

Analyzing the Message of the Speech

When an audience member listens to a speech, he or she should be attending to three fundamental **factors**: ideas, organization, and support. The most important thing to consider is whether the speaker's main ideas are *logical and clearly expressed.* If the ideas are comprehensible, an audience member can then consider whether they have been expressed in the *logical order*, or whether the speaker has presented them in a disorganized fashion. Finally, the audience member needs to consider whether the speaker's main ideas have been adequately *supported* by argument or factual evidence. Does the speaker provide enough support for his arguments to remain credible? Is the evidence provided relevant to the main ideas of the speech?

Reading

The Reading section of the TOEFL Essentials consists of a total of 30-45 questions which will last from 22-33 minutes.

There are four subsections of the Reading section.

Vocabulary

The vocabulary questions present you with a set of words and you must select the option closest in meaning.

General Reading

In this set of questions, you have to read a text you might encounter in everyday life and answer 2-4 questions about it.

Academic Reading: Tables

This set of questions requires you to read academic information in a table format and answer questions about the information.

Academic Reading: Passages

This is the most traditional set of questions. You will be given an academic passage to read, followed by a set of six questions.

Tips for the Reading Section

The reading section requires you to demonstrate your ability to find information, use basic comprehension, and read to learn.

Tip 1: Reading to Find Information

When reading to find specific ideas, it is important to be able to **scan** or **skim** a text for a specific phrase or context. To improve your reading speed and ability to scan a text, find passages that discuss a specific topic and practice looking for main ideas quickly without taking the time to read every word or sentence.

Tip 2: Basic Comprehension

When reading for basic comprehension of a passage, you will likely be asked to identify **themes, main ideas, and vocabulary** in context. These pieces of information are most likely to be found in the first sentence of the paragraph and in introductory or conclusion paragraphs. Spend some time reading through paragraphs and short stories looking for key information.

Tip 3: Reading to Learn

When reading to learn, one must be aware of **organization** and **presentation** of information within a passage. As you read through passages, try to identify the point of a passage, as well as whether it is speaking in an informative or persuasive manner. Keep track of important details, as some questions may require you to insert sentences that fit best in a passage. In these questions, there may be more than one answer that is technically correct, but only one that is truly the best fit.

Reading Comprehension Skills

This section is organized to introduce you to the passages that you will find on your exam. We cover the different types of passages from narrative to persuasive. Then, we move to the reason that a passage is written. As you may know, some texts are written to persuade. Other passages want to inform.

The writing devices used by writers are important to understand as you practice reading passages. The other parts of a passage we focus on are main ideas, supporting details, and themes. Then, we review making inferences and drawing conclusions. With this step-by-step guide, you will move to a higher score on your test.

Careful reading and thinking about a passage are important in every part of life. Work with this information by reading books, magazines, or newspapers. When you read carefully, you can use this information for other passages. With practice you will strengthen your skills for the future.

Types of Passages

A **narrative** passage is a story that can be fiction or nonfiction (i.e., false or true). To be a narrative, the passage must have a few things. First, the text must have a plot (i.e., an order of events). Some narratives are written in a clear order, but this is not necessary. If the narrative is good, then you will find the events interesting, regardless of the order in which they happen. Second, a narrative has characters. These characters can be people, animals, or even lifeless items. As long as they play in the plot, they are a character. Third, a narrative passage often has figurative language. This is a tool that authors use to stir the imagination of readers with comparisons or comments. For example, a metaphor is a comparison between two things without using the words *like* or *as*. *He stood like a king* is not an example of a metaphor. *The moon was a frosty snowball* is an example of a metaphor. In reality, the moon is not a snowball. Yet, the comparison gives a sense of calm to readers.

An **expository** passage aims to inform or teach readers. This type of passage is nonfiction and usually centers around an easily explained topic. Often, an expository passage has helpful organizing words: *first, next, for example*, and *therefore*. These words let readers know where they are in the passage. While expository passages don't need to have difficult vocabulary and fancy writing, they can be better with them. Yet, this can make it difficult to pay attention to an expository passage. Expository passages are not always about things that will interest you. Also, writers focus more on clearness and precision than with keeping the reader's interest. By careful reading, you will establish a good habit of focus when you read an expository passage.

Review Video: Expository Passages
Visit mometrix.com/academy and enter code: 256515

A **technical** passage is written to describe a complicated thing or action. Technical writing is common in medical and technology fields. In those fields, ideas of mathematics, science, and engineering need to be explained simply and clearly. A technical passage usually proceeds in a step-by-step order to help with understanding the passage. Technical passages often have clear headings and subheadings. These headings act like the organizing words in an expository passage: they let readers know where they are in a passage. Also, you will find that these passages divide sections by numbers or letters. Many technical passages look more like an outline than the paragraphs that you are reading right now. Depending on the audience, the amount of difficult vocabulary will change in a technical passage. Some technical passages try to stay away from language that readers will have to look up. However, some difficult vocabulary has to be used for writers to share their message.

Review Video: Technical Passages
Visit mometrix.com/academy and enter code: 478923

A **persuasive** passage is written to change the minds of readers so that they agree with the author. The purpose of the passage may be very clear or very difficult to find. A persuasive passage wants to make an acceptable argument and win the trust of the reader. In some cases, a persuasive passage will be similar to an informative passage. Both passages make an argument and offer supporting details. However, a persuasive passage is more likely to appeal to the reader's feelings and make arguments based on opinions. Persuasive passages may not describe other points of view. So, when they do show other points of view, they may show favoritism to one side.

Persuasive passages will focus on one main argument and make many minor arguments (i.e., arguments that help the main argument) along the way. If you are going to accept the main argument, then you need to accept the minor arguments. So, the main argument will only be as strong as the minor arguments. These arguments should be rooted in fact and experience, not opinions. The best persuasive passages give enough supporting detail to back up arguments without confusing readers. Remember that a fact must be open to independent verification (i.e., the fact must be something that can be backed up by someone else). Also, statistics (i.e., data or figures collected for study) are helpful only when they look at other choices. For example, a statistic on the number of bicycles sold would only be useful if it was taken over a limited time period and in a specific area. Good readers are careful with statistics because statistics can show what we want to see. Or, they can hide what we don't want to see. The writers of your test know that their passages will be met by questioning readers. So, your skill at questioning what you read will be a help in your exam.

Review Video: How to Write a Persuasive Essay
Visit mometrix.com/academy and enter code: 621428

Opinions come from how we feel and what we think. Persuasive writers often try to appeal to the emotions (i.e., use or influence someone's feelings) of readers to make their arguments. You should always ask questions about this approach. You should ask questions because an author can pull you into accepting something that you don't want to accept. Sometimes these appeals can be used fairly. For example, some subjects cannot be totally addressed without an appeal to a reader's feelings. Think about an article on drunk driving. Some examples in the article will alarm or sadden readers because of the terrible outcome.

On the other hand, appeals to feelings are unacceptable when they try to **mislead** readers. For example, a presidential candidate (i.e., someone running for president) says that he/she cares about the country. The candidate pushes you to make a connection. You care about the country as well and have positive feelings toward it. The candidate wants you to connect your positive feelings about the country with your thoughts about him or her. If you make more connections with the candidate, then you are likely to vote for him or her. Also, the person running for president hints that other candidates do not care about the country.

Another common and unacceptable appeal to feelings is the use of **loaded language**. Calling a religious person a *fanatic* or a person interested in the environment a *tree hugger* are examples of loaded language.

ORGANIZATION OF THE PASSAGE

The way a passage is organized can help readers to understand the author's purpose and conclusions. There are many ways to organize a passage, and each one has an important use.

Some nonfiction texts are organized to present a **problem** followed by a **solution**. For this type of passage, the problem is explained before the solution is given. When the problem is well known, the solution may be given in a few sentences at the beginning. Other passages may focus on the solution, and the problem will be talked about a few times. Some passages will outline many solutions to a problem. This will leave you to choose among the possible solutions. If authors have loyalty to one solution, they may not describe some of the other solutions. Be careful with the author's plan when reading a problem-solution passage. When you know the author's point of view, you can make a better judgment of the solution.

Sometimes authors will organize information clearly for you to follow and locate the information. However, this is not always the case with passages in an exam. Two common ways to order a passage are cause and effect and chronological order. When using **chronological order** (i.e., a plan that moves in order from the first step to the last), the author gives information in the order that the event happened. For example, biographies are written in chronological order. The person's birth and childhood are first. Their adult life is next. The events leading up to the person's death are last.

In **cause and effect** passages, an author shows one thing that makes something else happen. For example, if one were to go to bed very late and wake up very early, then they would be tired in the morning. The cause is a lack of sleep, with the effect of being tired the next day.

Finding the cause-and-effect relationships in a passage can be tricky. Often, these relationships come with certain words or terms. When authors use words like *because*, *since*, *in order*, and *so*, they are describing a cause and effect relationship. Think about the sentence: *He called her because he needed the homework*. This is a simple causal relationship. The cause was his need for the homework, and the effect was his phone call. Yet, not all cause and effect relationships are marked like this. Think about the sentences: *He called her. He needed the homework.* When the cause-and-effect relationship does not come with a keyword, the relationship can be known by asking why. For example, *He called her*. Why did he call her? The answer is in the next sentence: He needed the homework.

Review Video: Rhetorical Strategy of Cause-and-Effect Analysis
Visit mometrix.com/academy and enter code: 725944

When authors try to change the minds of readers, they may use cause-and-effect relationships. However, these relationships should not always be taken at face value. To read a persuasive essay well, you need to judge the cause-and-effect relationships. For example, imagine an author wrote the following: *The parking deck has not been making money because people want to ride their bikes.* The relationship is clear: the cause is that people want to ride their bikes. The effect is that the parking deck has not been making money. However, you should look at this argument again. Maybe there are other reasons that the parking deck was not a success: a bad economy, too many costs, etc.

Many passages follow the **compare-and-contrast** model. In this model, the similarities and differences between two ideas or things are reviewed. A review of the similarities between ideas is called comparison. In a perfect comparison, the author shows ideas or things in the same way. If authors want to show the similarities between football and baseball, they can list the equipment and rules for each game. Think about the similarities as they appear in the passage and take note of any differences.

Review Video: Compare and Contrast
Visit mometrix.com/academy and enter code: 798319

Careful thinking about ideas and conclusions can seem like a difficult task. You can make this task easy by understanding the basic parts of ideas and writing skills. Looking at the way that ideas link to others is a good way to begin. Sometimes authors will write about two opposing ideas. Other times, an author will support a topic, and another author will argue against the topic. The review of these rival ideas is known as **contrast**. In contrast, all ideas should be presented clearly. If the author does favor a side, you need to read carefully to find how the author shows or hides this favoritism. Also, as you read the passage, you should write out how one side views the other.

PURPOSES FOR WRITING

To be a careful reader, pay attention to the author's **position** and purpose. Even passages that seem fair and equal--like textbooks--have a position or bias (i.e., the author is unfair or inaccurate with opposing ideas). Readers need to take these positions into account when considering the author's message. Authors who appeal to feelings or favor one side of an argument make their position clear. Authors' positions may be found in what they write and in what they don't write. Normally, you would want to review other passages on the same topic to understand the author's position. However, you are in the middle of an exam. So, look for language and arguments that show a position.

Review Video: Author's Position
Visit mometrix.com/academy and enter code: 827954

Sometimes, finding the **purpose** of an author is easier than finding his or her position. In most cases, the author has no interest in hiding his or her purpose. A passage for entertainment will be written to please readers. Most stories are written to entertain. However, they can inform or persuade. Informative texts are easy to recognize. The most difficult purpose of a text to determine is persuasion. In persuasion, the author wants to make the purpose hard to find. When you learn that the author wants to persuade, you should be skeptical of the argument. Persuasive passages may try to establish an entertaining tone and hope to amuse you into agreement. On the other hand, an informative tone may be used to seem fair and equal to all sides.

An author's purpose is clear often in the organization of the text (e.g., section headings in bold font point to an informative passage). However, you may not have this organization in your passages. So, if authors make their main idea clear from the beginning, then their likely purpose is to inform. If the author makes a main argument and gives minor arguments for support, then the purpose is probably to persuade. If the author tells a story, then his or her purpose is most likely to entertain. If the author wants your attention more than to persuade or inform, then his or her purpose is most likely to entertain. You must judge authors on how well they reach their purpose. In other words, think about the type of passage (e.g., technical, persuasive, etc.) that the author has written and if the author has followed the demands of the passage type.

Review Video: Understanding the Author's Intent
Visit mometrix.com/academy and enter code: 511819

The author's purpose will influence his or her writing approach and the reader's reaction. In a **persuasive essay**, the author wants to prove something to readers. There are several important marks of bad persuasive writing. Opinion given as fact is one mark. When some authors try to persuade readers, they give their opinions as if they were facts. Readers must be on guard for statements that sound like facts but cannot be tested. Another mark of persuasive writing is the appeal to feelings. An author will try to play with the feelings of readers by appealing to their ideas of what is right and wrong. When an author uses strong language to excite the reader's feelings, then the author may want to persuade. Many times, a persuasive passage will give an unfair explanation of other sides. Or, the other sides are not shown.

An **informative passage** is written to teach readers. Informative passages are almost always nonfiction. The purpose of an informative passage is to share information in the clearest way. In an informative passage, you may have a thesis statement (i.e., an argument on the topic of a passage that is explained by proof). A thesis statement is a sentence that normally comes at end of the first paragraph. Authors of informative passages are likely to put more importance on being clear. Informative passages do not normally appeal to the feelings. They often contain facts and figures. Informative passages almost never include the opinion of the author. However, you should know that there can be a bias in the facts. Sometimes, a persuasive passage can be like an informative passage. This is true when authors give their ideas as if they were facts.

Entertainment passages describe real or imagined people, places, and events. Entertainment passages are often stories or poems. So, figurative language is a common part of these passages. Often, an entertainment passage appeals to the imagination and feelings. Authors may persuade or inform in an entertainment passage. Or, an entertainment passage may cause readers to think differently about a subject.

When authors want to **share feelings,** they may use strong language. Authors may share feelings about a moment of great pain or happiness. Other times, authors will try to persuade readers by sharing feelings. Some phrases like *I felt* and *I sense* hint that the author is sharing feelings. Authors may share a story of deep pain or great joy. You must not be influenced by these stories. You need to keep some distance to judge the author's argument.

Almost all writing is descriptive. In one way or another, authors try to describe events, ideas, or people. Some texts are concerned only with **description**. A descriptive passage focuses on a single subject and seeks to explain the subject clearly. Descriptive passages contain many adjectives and adverbs (i.e., words that give a complete picture for you to imagine). Normally, a descriptive passage is informative. Yet, the passage may be persuasive or entertaining.

Writing Devices

Authors will use different writing devices to make their message clear for readers. One of those devices is comparison and contrast. As mentioned above, when authors show how two things are alike, they are **comparing** them. When authors describe how two things are different, they are **contrasting** them. The compare and contrast passage is a common part of nonfiction. Comparisons are known by certain words or phrases: *both*, *same*, *like*, *too*, and *as well*. Contrasts may have words or phrases like *but*, *however*, *on the other hand*, *instead*, and *yet*. Of course, comparisons and contrasts may be understood without using those words or phrases. A single sentence may compare and contrast. Think about the sentence *Brian and Sheila love ice cream, but Brian loves vanilla and Sheila loves strawberry*. In one sentence, the author has described both a similarity (love of ice cream) and a difference (favorite flavor).

Another regular writing device is **cause and effect**. A cause is an act or event that makes something happen. An effect is what results from the cause. A cause and effect relationship is not always easy to find. So, there are some words and phrases that show causes: *since*, *because*, and *due to*. Words and phrases that show effects include *consequently, therefore, this lead(s) to, as a result*. For example, *Because the sky was clear, Ron did not bring an umbrella*. The cause is the clear sky, and the effect is that Ron did not bring an umbrella. Readers may find that the cause and effect relationship is not clear. For example, *He was late and missed the meeting*. This does not have any words that show cause or effect. Yet, the sentence still has a cause (e.g., he was late) and an effect (e.g., he missed the meeting).

Remember the chance for a single cause to have many effects. (e.g., *Single cause*: Because you left your homework on the table, your dog eats the homework. *Many effects*: (1) As a result, you fail your homework. (2) Your parents do not let you see your friends. (3) You miss out on the new movie. (4) You miss holding the hand of an important person.)

Also, a **single effect** can have many causes. For example, a single-effect sentence is: *Alan has a fever*. This fever can have multiple causes: 1) An unexpected cold front came through the area. (2) Alan forgot to take his multi-vitamin.

An effect can also become the cause of another effect. This is known as a **cause and effect chain**. For example: *As a result of her hatred for not doing work, Lynn got ready for her exam*. This led to her passing her test with high marks. Hence, her resume was accepted, and her application was also accepted.

Often, authors use analogies to add meaning to their passages. An **analogy** is a comparison of two things. The words in the analogy are connected by a relationship. Look at this analogy: *moo is to cow as quack is to duck*. This analogy compares the sound that a cow makes with the sound that a duck makes. What could you do if the word *quack* was not given? Well, you could finish the analogy if you know the connection between *moo* and *cow*. Relationships for analogies include synonyms, antonyms, part to whole, definition, and actor to action.

Point of view has an important influence on a passage. A passage's point of view is how the author or a character sees or thinks about things. A point of view influences the events of a passage, the meetings among characters, and the ending to the story. For example, two characters watch a child ride a bike. Character one watches outside. Character two watches from inside a house. Both see the same event, yet they are around different noises, sights, and smells. Character one may see different things that happen outside that character two cannot see from inside. Also, point of view can be influenced by past events and beliefs. For example, if character one loves bikes, then she will remember how proud she is of the child. If character two is afraid of riding bikes, then he may not remember the event or may fear for the child's safety.

In fiction, the two main points of view are **first person** and **third person**. The *narrator* is the person who tells a story's events. The *protagonist* is the main character of a story. If the narrator is the protagonist in a story, then the story is written in first-person. In first person, the author writes from the view of *I*. Third-person point of view is the most common among stories. With third person, authors refer to each character by using *he* or *she* and the narrator is not involved in the story. In third-person omniscient, the narrator is not a character in the story and tells the story of all of the characters at the same time.

Review Video: Point of View
Visit mometrix.com/academy and enter code: 383336

Transitional words and phrases are devices that guide readers through a passage. You may know the common transitions, though you may not have thought about how they are used. Some transitional phrases (*after, before, during, in the middle of*) give information about time. Some hint that an example is about to be given (*for example, in fact, for instance*). Writers use transitions to compare (*also, likewise*) and contrast (*however, but, yet*). Transitional words and phrases can point to addition (*and, also, furthermore, moreover*) and understood relationships (*if, then, therefore, as a result, since*). Finally, transitional words and phrases can separate the chronological steps (*first, second, last*).

Review Video: Transition Words
Visit mometrix.com/academy and enter code: 707563

Understanding a Passage

One of the most important skills in reading comprehension is finding **topics** and **main ideas.** There is a small difference between these two. The topic is the *subject* of a passage (what the passage is all about). The main idea is the most important *argument* being made by the author. The topic is shared in a few words while the main idea needs a full sentence to be understood. As an example, a short passage might have the topic of penguins, and the main idea could be written as *Penguins are different from other birds in many ways.*

In most nonfiction writing, the topic and the main idea will be stated clearly. Sometimes, they will come in a sentence at the very beginning or end of the passage. When you want to know the topic, you frequently find it in the first sentence of each paragraph. A body paragraph's first sentence is often--but not always--the topic sentence. The topic sentence gives you a summary of the ideas in the paragraph. You may find that the topic or main idea is not given clearly. So, you must read every sentence of the passage. Then, try to come up with an overall idea from each sentence.

Note: A thesis statement is not the same as the main idea. The main idea gives a brief, general summary of a text. The thesis statement gives a clear idea on an issue that is backed up with evidence.

Review Video: Topics and Main Ideas
Visit mometrix.com/academy and enter code: 407801

Passage Structure for Non-Narrative Passages

Title

Centered on the page, the title's main words are capitalized (articles, prepositions, and infinitives are not capitalized in a title). The title may have quotation marks, or it may be underlined or italicized. The title has a few words that hint at the subject of the paper and catch the reader's interest.

Introduction

An introduction summarizes the passage and the thesis statement. The purpose of the introduction is to grab the reader's attention. To do this, authors may use a quote, question, or strong opinion. Some authors choose to use an interesting description or puzzling statement. Also, authors use the introduction to explain their reason for writing.

Body Paragraph

Following the introduction, body paragraphs are used to explain the thesis statement. A body paragraph has a topic sentence, typically the first sentence. In these paragraphs, there is evidence that helps the argument of the paragraph. Also, the author may give commentary on the evidence. Be careful because this commentary can be filled with bias.

The topic sentence gives the paragraph's subject and the main idea. The rest of the body paragraph should be linked to the topic sentence. Again, the topic sentence should be supported with facts, details, and examples.

The topic sentence is general and covers the ideas in a body paragraph. Sometimes, the topic sentence may be implied (i.e., the sentence is not stated directly by the author). Also, the topic sentence shows the connections among the supporting details.

Conclusion

The conclusion should provide a summary on the passage. New material is not given in the conclusion. The conclusion is the final paragraph that may have a call to action (something the writer wants readers to do) or a question for the reader to think about.

The main idea is the umbrella argument of a passage. So, **supporting details** back up the main idea. To show that a main idea is correct, authors add details that prove their idea. All passages contain details. However, they are referred to as supporting details when they help an argument in the passage. Supporting details are found in informative and persuasive texts. Sometimes they will come with terms like *for example* or *for instance*. Or, they will be numbered with terms like *first*, *second*, and *last*. You should think about how the author's supporting details back up his or her main idea. Supporting details can be correct, yet they may help the author's main idea. Sometimes supporting details can seem helpful. However, they may be useless when they are based on opinions.

Review Video: Supporting Details
Visit mometrix.com/academy and enter code: 396297

An example of a main idea is: *Giraffes live in the Serengeti of Africa*. A supporting detail about giraffes could be: *A giraffe in the Serengeti benefits from a long neck by reaching twigs and leaves on tall trees.* The main idea gives the general idea that the text is about giraffes. The supporting detail gives a clear fact about how the giraffes eat.

A **theme** is an issue, an idea, or a question raised by a passage. For example, a theme of *Cinderella* is determination as Cinderella serves her stepsisters and stepmother. Passages may have many themes, so be careful to find only themes that you are asked to find. One common mark of themes is that they give more questions than answers. Authors try to push readers to consider themes in other ways. You can find themes by asking about the general problems that the passage is addressing. A good way to find a theme is to begin reading with a question in mind (e.g., How does this passage use the theme of love?) and to look for answers to that question.

Review Video: Themes in Literature
Visit mometrix.com/academy and enter code: 732074

Evaluating a Passage

When you read informational passages, you need to make a conclusion from the author's writing. You can **identify a logical conclusion** (i.e., find a conclusion that makes sense) to know whether you agree or disagree with an author. Coming to this conclusion is like making an inference. You combine the information from the passage with what you already know. From the passage's information and your knowledge, you can come to a conclusion that makes sense. One way to have a conclusion that makes sense is to take notes of all the author's points. When the notes are organized, they may point to the logical conclusion. Another way to reach conclusions is to ask if the author's passage raises any helpful questions. Sometimes you will be able to draw many conclusions from a passage. Yet, some of these may be conclusions that were never imagined by the author. Therefore, find reasons in the passage for the conclusions that you make.

Review Video: How to Support a Conclusion
Visit mometrix.com/academy and enter code: 281653

Text evidence is the information that supports a main argument or minor argument. This evidence, or proof, can lead you to a conclusion. Information used as text evidence is clear, descriptive, and full of facts. Supporting details give evidence to back up an argument.

For example, a passage may state that winter occurs during opposite months in the Northern hemisphere (north of the equator) and Southern hemisphere (south of the equator). Text evidence for this claim may include a list of countries where winter occurs in opposite months. Also, you may be given reasons that winter occurs at different times of the year in these hemispheres (such as the tilt of the earth as it rotates around the sun).

Review Video: Textual Evidence
Visit mometrix.com/academy and enter code: 486236

A text is **credible**, or believable, when the author is knowledgeable and fair. The author's motivations for writing the passage have an important part in knowing the credibility of the passage. For example, passages written about a professional soccer game by a sports reporter and one written by an average fan will have different levels of credibility.

Review Video: Author Credibility
Visit mometrix.com/academy and enter code: 827257

A reader should always draw **conclusions** from passages. Sometimes conclusions are implied (i.e., information that is assumed) from written information. Other times the information is **stated directly** within the passage. You should try to draw conclusions from information stated in a passage. Furthermore, you should always read through the entire passage before drawing conclusions. Readers often expect the author's conclusions at the beginning or the end of the passage. However, many texts do not follow this format.

Implications are things that the author does not say directly, but you can assume from what the author does say. For example: *I stepped outside and opened my umbrella. By the time I got to work, the cuffs of my pants were soaked*. The author never says that it is raining. However, you can conclude that this information is implied. Conclusions from implications must be well supported by the passage. To draw a conclusion, you should have many pieces of proof. If you have only one piece of evidence, then you need to be sure that there is no other possible explanation than your conclusion. Practice drawing conclusions from implications in real life events to improve your skills.

Outlining the information in a passage should be a familiar skill to readers. A good outline will show the pattern of the passage and lead to better conclusions. A common outline lists the main ideas of the passage in the order that they come. Then, beneath each main idea, you can list the minor ideas and details. An outline does not need to include every detail from the passage. However, the outline should show everything that is important to the argument.

Another helpful tool is **summarizing** information. This process is similar to creating an outline. First, a summary should define the main idea of the passage. The summary should have the most important supporting details or arguments. Summaries can be unclear or wrong because they do not stay true to the information in the passage. A helpful summary should have the same message as the passage.

Ideas from a passage can be organized using **graphic organizers**. A graphic organizer reduces information to a few key points. A graphic organizer like a timeline may have an event listed for each date on the timeline. However, an outline may have an event listed under a key point that happens in the passage.

Make a graphic organizer that works best for you. Whatever helps you remember information from a passage is what you need to use. A spider-map is another example. This map takes a main idea from the story and places it in a bubble. From one main idea bubble, you put supporting points that connect to the main idea. A Venn diagram groups information as separate or connected with some overlap.

Review Video: Graphic Organizers
Visit mometrix.com/academy and enter code: 665513

Paraphrasing is another method that you can use to understand a passage. To paraphrase, you put what you have read into your own words. Or, you can *translate* what the author shared into your words by including as many details as you can.

Responding to a Passage

One part of being a good reader is making predictions. A **prediction** is a guess about what will happen next. Readers make predictions from what they have read and what they already know. For example: *Staring at the computer screen in shock, Kim reached for the glass of water.* The sentence leaves you to think that she is not looking at the glass. So, you may guess that Kim is going to knock over the glass. Yet in the next sentence you may read that Kim does not knock over the glass. As you have more information, be ready for your predictions to change.

Review Video: Predictive Reading
Visit mometrix.com/academy and enter code: 437248

Test-taking tip: To respond to questions that ask about predictions, your answer should come from the passage.

You will be asked to understand text that gives ideas without stating them directly. An **inference** is something that is implied but not stated directly by the author. For example: *After the final out of the inning, the fans were filled with joy and rushed the field.* From this sentence, you can infer that the fans were watching baseball and their team won. You should not use information outside of the passage before making inferences. As you practice making inferences, you will find that they need all of your attention.

Review Video: Inference
Visit mometrix.com/academy and enter code: 379203

Test-taking tip: When asked about inferences, look for **context clues**. Context is what surrounds the words and sentences, adding explanation or information to an unknown piece. An answer can be *true* but not *correct*. The context clues will help you find the answer that is best. When asked for the implied meaning of a statement, you should locate the statement first. Then, read the context around the statement. Finally, look for an answer with a similar phrase.

For your exam, you must be able to find a text's **sequence** (i.e., the order that things happen). When the sequence is very important to the author, the passage comes with signal words: *first, then, next,* and *last.* However, a sequence can be implied. For example, *He walked through the garden and gave water and fertilizer to the plants.* Clearly, the man did not walk through the garden at the beginning. First, he found water. Then, he collected fertilizer. Next, he walked through the garden. Finally, he gave water and fertilizer to the plants. Passages do not always come in a clear sequence. Sometimes they begin at the end. Or, they can begin halfway through and then start over at the beginning. You can strengthen your understanding of the passage by taking notes to understand the sequence.

Dual passages, or comparative essays, give two passages from authors with different points of view. The format of the two passages will change with each exam. For example, the author of the first passage may give an idea from his or her point of view. The author of the second passage gives an argument against the first passage. Other dual passages will give a topic in the first passage. Then the second passage will help or provide explanation to the topic in the first passage.

You may see that the questions ask about passage one, passage two, and both passages. No matter the length or kind of passages, you should read them in order (read Passage 1 first, then move on to Passage 2). However, if your time is limited, you can read passage 1 first and answer all of the questions for passage 1. Then, read passage 2 and answer the remaining questions.

Building a Vocabulary

Learning the basics of language is helpful in understanding what you read. **Structural analysis** means to break a word into pieces to find its definition. Parts of a word include prefixes, suffixes, and root words. Knowing the meanings of these parts can help you understand the definition of a difficult word.

The main part of a word is known as the root. Prefixes are common letter combinations at the beginning of words. Suffixes are common letter combinations at the ends of words. In pieces, a word looks like this: prefix + root word + suffix. First, look at the individual definitions of the root word, prefix, and/or suffix. Then, see how they add to the root. You can use knowledge of a prefix's and/or suffix's definition to determine a close definition of the word. For example, if you don't know the definition of *uninspired* you may be able to figure it out because you know that *un-* means 'not.' Thus, the full word means *not inspired*. Learning the common prefixes and suffixes can help you define difficult words.

Review Video: Determining Word Meanings
Visit mometrix.com/academy and enter code: 894894

Below is a list of common prefixes and their meanings:

PREFIXES FOR NUMBERS

Prefix	Definition	Examples
Bi-	Two	bisect, biennial, bicycle
Mono-	One, single	monogamy, monologue, monopoly
Poly-	Many	polymorphous, polygamous, polygon
Semi-	Half, partly	semicircle, semicolon, semiannually
Uni-	one	uniform, unity, unanimous
a-	in, on, of, up, to	abed, afoot
ab-	from, away, off	abdicate, abjure
ad-	to, toward	advance, adventure
ante-	before, previous	antecedent, antedate
anti-	against, opposing	antipathy, antidote
cata-	down, away, thorou	catastrophe, cataclysm
circum-	around	circumspect, circumference
com-	with, together, very	commotion, complicate
contra-	against, opposing	contradict, contravene
de-	from	depart
dia-	through, across, apa	diameter, diagnose
dis-	away, off, down, not	dissent, disappear
epi-	upon	epilogue
ex-	out	extract, excerpt
hypo-	under, beneath	hypodermic, hypothesis
inter-	among, between	intercede, interrupt
intra-	within	intramural, intrastate
ob-	against, opposing	objection
per-	through	perceive, permit
peri-	around	periscope, perimeter
post-	after, following	postpone, postscript
pre-	before, previous	prevent, preclude
pro-	forward, in place of	propel, pronoun
retro-	back, backward	retrospect, retrograde
sub-	under, beneath	subjugate, substitute
super-	above, extra	supersede, supernumerar
trans-	across, beyond, ove	transact, transport
ultra-	beyond, excessively	ultramodern, ultrasonic

PREFIXES FOR TIME, DIRECTION, AND SPACE

Prefix	Definition	Examples
a-	in, on, of, up, to	abed, afoot
ab-	from, away, off	abdicate, abjure
ad-	to, toward	advance, adventure
ante-	before, previous	antecedent, antedate
anti-	against, opposing	antipathy, antidote
cata-	down, away, thorou	catastrophe, cataclysm
circum	around	circumspect, circumferen
com-	with, together, very	commotion, complicate
contra-	against, opposing	contradict, contravene
de-	from	depart
dia-	through, across, apa	diameter, diagnose
dis-	away, off, down, not	dissent, disappear
epi-	upon	epilogue
ex-	out	extract, excerpt
hypo-	under, beneath	hypodermic, hypothesis
inter-	among, between	intercede, interrupt
intra-	within	intramural, intrastate
ob-	against, opposing	objection
per-	through	perceive, permit
peri-	around	periscope, perimeter
post-	after, following	postpone, postscript
pre-	before, previous	prevent, preclude
pro-	forward, in place of	propel, pronoun
retro-	back, backward	retrospect, retrograde
sub-	under, beneath	subjugate, substitute
super-	above, extra	supersede, supernumera
trans-	across, beyond, over	transact, transport
ultra-	beyond, excessively	ultramodern, ultrasonic

Negative Prefixes

Prefix	Definition	Examples
a-	without, lacking	atheist, agnostic
in-	not, opposing	incapable, ineligible
non-	not	nonentity, nonsense
un-	not, reverse of	unhappy, unlock

Extra Prefixes

Prefix	Definition	Examples
belli-	war, warlike	bellicose
bene-	well, good	benefit, benefactor
equi-	equal	equivalent, equilibrium
for-	away, off, from	forget, forswear
fore-	previous	foretell, forefathers
homo-	same, equal	homogenized, homonym
hyper-	excessive, over	hypercritical, hypertension
in-	in, into	intrude, invade
magn-	large	magnitude, magnify
mal-	bad, poorly, not	malfunction, malpractice
mis-	bad, poorly, not	misspell, misfire
mor-	death	mortality, mortuary
neo-	new	Neolithic, neoconservative
omni-	all, everywhere	omniscient, omnivore
ortho-	right, straight	orthogonal, orthodox
over-	above	overbearing, oversight
pan-	all, entire	panorama, pandemonium
para-	beside, beyond	parallel, paradox
phil-	love, like	philosophy, philanthropic
prim-	first, early	primitive, primary
re-	backward, again	revoke, recur
sym-	with, together	sympathy, symphony
vis-	to see	visage, visible

Below is a list of common suffixes and their meanings:

Adjective Suffixes

Suffix	Definition	Examples
-able (-ible)	capable of being	toler*able*, ed*ible*
-esque	in the style of, like	picturesque, grotesque
-ful	filled with, marked by	thankful, zestful
-ific	make, cause	terrific, beatific
-ish	suggesting, like	churlish, childish
-less	lacking, without	hopeless, countless
-ous	marked by, given to	religious, riotous

Noun Suffixes

Suffix	Definition	Examples
-acy	state, condition	accuracy, privacy
-ance	act, condition, fact	acceptance, vigilance
-ard	one that does excessively	drunkard, sluggard
-ation	action, state, result	occupation, starvation
-dom	state, rank, condition	serfdom, wisdom
-er (-or)	office, action	teach*er*, elevat*or*, hon*or*
-ess	feminine	waitress, duchess
-hood	state, condition	manhood, statehood
-ion	action, result, state	union, fusion
-ism	act, manner, doctrine	barbarism, socialism
-ist	worker, follower	monopolist, socialist
-ity (-ty)	state, quality, condition	acid*ity*, civil*ity*, twen*ty*
-ment	result, action	Refreshment
-ness	quality, state	greatness, tallness
-ship	position	internship, statesmanship
-sion (-tion)	state, result	revi*sion*, expedi*tion*
-th	act, state, quality	warmth, width
-tude	quality, state, result	magnitude, fortitude

Verb Suffixes

Suffix	Definition	Examples
-ate	having, showing	separate, desolate
-en	cause to be, become	deepen, strengthen
-fy	make, cause to have	glorify, fortify
-ize	cause to be, treat with	sterilize, mechanize

There is more to a word than its dictionary definition. The **denotative** meaning of a word is the actual meaning found in a dictionary. For example, a house and a home are places where people live. The **connotative meaning** is what comes to mind when you think of a word. For example, a house may be a simple, solid building. Yet, a home may be a comfortable, welcoming place where a family lives. Most non-fiction is fact-based with no use of figurative language. So, you can assume that the writer will use denotative meanings. In fiction, drama, and poetry, the author may use the connotative meaning. Use context clues to know if the author is using the denotative or connotative meaning of a word.

Review Video: Connotation and Denotation
Visit mometrix.com/academy and enter code: 310092

Readers of all levels will find new words in passages. The best way to define a word in **context** is to think about the words that are around the unknown word. For example, nouns that you don't know may be followed by examples that give a definition. Think about this example: *Dave arrived at the party in hilarious garb: a leopard-print shirt, buckskin pants, and tennis shoes.* If you didn't know the meaning of garb, you could read the examples (i.e., a leopard-print shirt, buckskin pants, and tennis shoes) and know that *garb* means *clothing*. Examples will not always be this clear. Try another example: *Parsley, lemon, and flowers were just a few of the items he used as garnishes.* The word *garnishes* is explained by parsley, lemon, and flowers. From this one sentence, you may know that the items are used for decoration. Are they decorating a food plate or an ice table with meat? You would need the other sentences in the paragraph to know for sure.

Review Video: Reading Comprehension: Using Context Clues
Visit mometrix.com/academy and enter code: 613660

Also, you can use contrasts to define an unfamiliar word in context. In many sentences, authors will not describe the unfamiliar word directly. Instead, they will describe the opposite of the unfamiliar word. So, you are given some information that will bring you closer to defining the word. For example: *Despite his intelligence, Hector's bad posture made him look obtuse. Despite* means that Hector's posture is at odds with his intelligence. The author explains that Hector's posture does not prove his intelligence. So, *obtuse* must mean *unintelligent*. Another example: *Even with the horrible weather, we were beatific about our trip to Alaska*. The weather is described as *horrible*. So, *beatific* must mean something positive.

Sometimes, there will be very few context clues to help you define an unknown word. When this happens, **substitution** is a helpful tool. First, try to think of some synonyms for the words. Then, use those synonyms in place of the unknown words. If the passage makes sense, then the substitution has given some information about the unknown word. For example: *Frank's admonition rang in her ears as she climbed the mountain.* If you don't know the definition of *admonition*, try some substitutions: *vow, promise, advice, complaint*, or *compliment*. These words hint that an *admonition* is some sort of message. Once in a while substitution can get you a precise definition.

Usually you can define an unfamiliar word by looking at the descriptive words in the context. For example: *Fred dragged the recalcitrant boy, kicking and screaming, up the stairs.* The words *dragged, kicking*, and *screaming* all hint that the boy hates going up the stairs. So, you may deduce that *recalcitrant* means something like unwilling or protesting. In this example, an unfamiliar adjective was identified. Contrasts do not always give detailed information about the unknown word. However, they do give you some clues to understand it.

Description is used more to define an unfamiliar noun than unfamiliar adjectives. For example: *Don's wrinkled frown and constantly shaking fist labeled him as a curmudgeon.* Don is described as having a *wrinkled frown* and *constantly shaking fist*. This hints that a *curmudgeon* must be a grumpy, old man.

Many words have more than one **definition**. So you may not know how the word is being used in a sentence. For example, the verb *cleave* can mean *join* or *separate*. When you see this word, you need to pick the definition that makes the most sense. For example: *The birds cleaved together as they flew from the oak tree.* The use of the word *together* hints that *cleave* is being used to mean *join*. Another example: *Hermione's knife cleaved the bread cleanly*. A knife cannot join bread together. So, the word must hint at separation. Learning the purpose of a word with many meanings needs the same tricks as defining an unknown word. Look for context clues and try substituting words.

To learn more from a passage, you need to understand how words connect to each other. This is done with understanding **synonyms** (e.g., words that mean the same thing) and **antonyms** (e.g., the opposite meaning of a word). For example, *dry* and *arid* are synonyms. However, *dry* and *wet* are antonyms. There are pairs of words in English that can be called synonyms, yet they have somewhat different definitions. For example, *friendly* and *collegial* can be used to describe a warm, close relationship. So, you would be correct to call them synonyms. However, *collegial* (linked to *colleague*) is used for professional or academic relationships. *Friendly* is not linked to professional or academic relationships.

Words should not be called synonyms when their differences are too great. For example, *hot* and *warm* are not synonyms because their meanings are too different. How do you know when two words are synonyms? First, try to replace one word for the other word. Then, be sure that the meaning of the sentence has not changed. Replacing *warm* for *hot* in a sentence gives a different meaning. *Warm* and *hot* may seem close in meaning. Yet *warm* means that the temperature is normal, while *hot* means that the temperature is very high.

Antonyms are words with opposite meanings. *Light* and *dark*, *up* and *down*, *right* and *left*, *good* and *bad* are sets of antonyms. However, there is a difference between antonyms and pairs of words that are different. *Black* and *gray* are not antonyms, because *black* is not the opposite of *gray*. On the other hand, *black* and *white* are antonyms. Not every word has an antonym. For example, many nouns do not have an antonym. What would be the antonym of *chair*?

During your exam, the questions about antonyms are likely to be about adjectives. Remember that adjectives are words that describe a noun. Some common adjectives include *red*, *fast*, *skinny*, and *sweet*. From these four adjectives, *red* is the one that does not have an antonym.

Review Video: What are Synonyms and Antonyms?
Visit mometrix.com/academy and enter code: 105612

Writing

You will have 34-30 minutes to complete writing section. The writing section includes 14-18 **build-a-sentence** questions in which you have to rearrange parts of a sentence to put them in the correct order. Then, you will be given a writing task in which you have to write an email to meet a specific purpose, then you will be given a second writing task to either describe a photo for a social media post or write a short forum post defending an opinion about an academic topic.

In each task, a topic will be presented to you and you must write out a discussion on it within the time allowed. You must evaluate the topic, organize your ideas, and develop them into a cohesive and coherent response.

The writing tasks will not necessarily have a right or a wrong answer. You will be scored on how well you are able to utilize standard written English, organize and explain your thoughts, and support those thoughts with reasons and examples.

Tips for the Writing Section

For the writing section of this test, you will need to answer an integrated writing task, which involves a reading or speaking comprehension section with a writing response to the topic. The Independent writing task asks you to explain and support your own opinion about an issue.

TIP 1: INTEGRATED WRITING TASK

For the integrated writing task, you will need to understand and respond to written and **verbal input**. Try to take note of what is said so you can refer back to this information in your own responses for comparison or contrast.

TIP 2: INDEPENDENT WRITING TASK

For the independent writing task, you will need to write an essay explaining and supporting your own **opinion** regarding a subject. For this, you should try to be as organized as possible, making clear points and organizing them into meaningful paragraphs. Follow the introduction, body, and conclusion format if possible. Practice discussing common issues in this format and review your work to eliminate unnecessary information. Remember that extra information only slows down and can confuse readers.

TIP 3: GENERAL RECOMMENDATIONS

Try to learn **descriptive adverbs and adjectives** that can be used in many arguments rather than using common words. Descriptive language can keep readers engaged and provide more detail if used correctly. Practice using a **QWERTY keyboard**, which you will need to use during this test.

The Writing Process

BRAINSTORM

Spend the first few minutes brainstorming ideas. Write down any ideas you might have on the topic. The purpose is to extract from the recesses of your memory any **relevant information**. In this stage, anything goes down. Write down any idea, regardless of how good or bad it may initially seem. You can use either the scratch paper provided or the word processor to quickly jot down your thoughts and ideas. The word processor is highly recommended though, particularly if you are a fast typist.

Strength through Diversity

The best papers will contain **diversity** of examples and reasoning. As you brainstorm, consider different perspectives. Not only are there two sides to every topic, but there are also countless **perspectives** that can be considered. On any topic, different groups are impacted, with many reaching the same conclusion or position, but through vastly different paths. Try to "see" the topic through as many different eyes as you can. Look at it from every angle and vantage point. The more diverse the reasoning used, the more balanced the paper will become and the better the score will be.

Example:

The topic of free trade is not just two-sided. It impacts politicians, domestic (US) manufacturers, foreign manufacturers, the US economy, the world economy, strategic alliances, retailers, wholesalers, consumers, unions, workers, and the exchange not only of goods, but also of ideas, beliefs, and cultures. The more of these angles that you can use to approach the topic, the more solid your reasoning and the stronger your position.

Furthermore, don't just use information as to how the topic impacts other people. Draw liberally from your own **experience and observations**. Describe a personal experience that you have had and your own emotions from that moment. Anything you've seen in your community or observed in society can be expanded upon to further round out your position on the topic.

Once you have finished with your creative flow, stop and **review** it. Which idea allowed you to come up with the most supporting information? It's extremely important that you pick an angle that will allow you to have a thorough and comprehensive coverage of the topic. This is not about your personal convictions, but about writing a concise, rational discussion of an idea.

Every garden of ideas gets weeds in it. The ideas that you brainstormed are going to be random pieces of information of mixed value. Go through them methodically and pick out the ones that are the best. The best ideas are **strong points** that you can easily write a few sentences or a paragraph about.

Now that you know which ideas you are going to use and focus on, **organize** them. Put your writing points in a logical order. You have your main ideas that you will focus on, and must align them in a sequence that will flow in a smooth, sensible path from point to point, so that the reader will go smoothly from one idea to the next in a logical path. Readers must have a sense of continuity as they read your paper. You don't want a paper that rambles back and forth.

Start Your Engines

You have a logical flow of main ideas with which to start writing. Begin **expanding** on the topics in the sequence that you have set for yourself. Pace yourself. Don't spend too much time on any one of the ideas that you are expanding on. You want to have time for all of them. Make sure you watch your time. If you have twenty minutes left to write out your ideas and you have ten ideas, then you can only use two minutes per idea. It can be a daunting task to cram a lot of information down in words in a short amount of time, but if you pace yourself, you can get through it all. If you find that you are falling behind, speed up. Move through each idea more quickly, spending less time to expand upon the idea in order to catch up.

Once you finish expanding on each idea, go back to your brainstorming session up above, where you wrote out your ideas. Go ahead and scratch through the ideas as you write about them. This will let you see what you need to write about next, and also allow you to pace yourself and see what you have left to cover.

Your first paragraph should have several easily identifiable features.

- First, it should have a quick **description** or paraphrasing of the topic. Use your own words to briefly explain what the topic is about.
- Second, you should explain your **opinion** of the topic and give an explanation of why you feel that way. What is your decision or conclusion on the topic?
- Third, you should list your "writing points." What are the **main ideas** that you came up with earlier? This is your opportunity to outline the rest of your paper. Write a sentence explaining each idea that will be explained in further depth in additional paragraphs. If someone were only to read this paragraph, he or she should be able to get a good summary of the entire paper.

Each of your successive paragraphs should expand on one of the points listed in the main paragraph. Use your personal experience and knowledge to support each of your points. Everything should be backed up by **examples**.

Once you have finished expanding upon each of your main points, wrap it up. **Summarize** what you have said in a conclusion paragraph. Explain your opinion of the topic once more and quickly review why you feel that way. At this stage, you have already backed up your statements, so there is no need to do that again. All you are doing is refreshing the reader's mind on your main points.

PUNCTUATION

If a section of text has an opening dash, parentheses, or comma at the beginning of a phrase, then you can be sure there should be a matching closing dash, parentheses, or comma at the end of the phrase. If items in a series are each separated by commas, then any additional items in that series will also need commas. Do not alternate punctuation. If a dash is at the beginning of a statement, then do not put a parenthesis at the ending of the statement.

WORD CONFUSION

"Which" should be used to refer to things only.

John's dog, which was called Max, is large and fierce.

"That" may be used to refer to either persons or things.

Is this the only book that Louis L'Amour wrote?

Is Louis L'Amour the author that [or who] wrote Western novels?

"Who" should be used to refer to persons only.

Mozart was the composer who [or that] wrote those operas.

PRONOUN USAGE

To determine the correct pronoun form in a compound subject, try each subject separately with the verb, adapting the form as necessary. Your ear will tell you which form is correct.

Example: *Bob and (I, me) will be going.*

Restate the sentence twice, using each subject individually. Bob will be going. I will be going. "Me will be going" does not make sense.

When a pronoun is immediately followed by a noun (as in "we boys"), say the sentence without the added noun. Your ear will tell you the correct pronoun form.

Example: (*We/Us) boys played football last year.*

Restate the sentence twice, without the noun. We played football last year. Us played football last year. Clearly "We played football last year" makes more sense.

Using Commas

Flow

Commas break the flow of text. To test whether they are necessary, read the text to yourself and pause for a moment at each comma. If the pauses seem natural, then the commas are correct. If they are not, then the commas are not correct.

Nonessential clauses and phrases

A comma should be used to set off **nonessential** clauses and participial phrases from the rest of the sentence. To determine if a clause is **essential**, remove it from the sentence. If the removal of the clause would alter the meaning of the sentence, then it is essential. Otherwise, it is nonessential.

Example: *John Smith, who was a disciple of Andrew Collins, was a noted archeologist.*

In the example above, the sentence describes John Smith's fame in archeology. The fact that he was a disciple of Andrew Collins is not necessary to that meaning. Therefore, separating it from the rest of the sentence with commas is correct.

Do not use a comma if the clause or phrase is essential to the meaning of the sentence.

Example: *Anyone who appreciates obscure French poetry will enjoy reading the book.*

If the phrase "who appreciates obscure French poetry" is removed, the sentence indicates that anyone would enjoy reading the book, not just those with an appreciation for obscure French poetry. However, the sentence implies that the book's enjoyment may not be for everyone, so the phrase is essential.

Another, perhaps easier, way to determine if the clause is essential is to see if it has a comma at its beginning or end. Consistent, parallel punctuation must be used, and so if you can determine a comma exists at one side of the clause, then you can be certain that a comma should exist on the opposite side.

Independent clauses

Use a comma before the words *and, but, or, nor, for,* or *yet* when they join independent clauses. To determine if two clauses are independent, remove the word that joins them. If each clause can stand alone as a complete sentence, then they are independent and need a comma between them.

Example: *He ran down the street, and then he ran over the bridge.*

He ran down the street. Then he ran over the bridge. Both clauses are capable of being their own sentence. Therefore, a comma must be used along with the word "and" to join the two clauses together.

If one or more of the clauses would be a fragment if left alone, then it must be joined to another clause and a comma is not needed between them.

Example: *He ran down the street and over the bridge.*

He ran down the street. Over the bridge. "Over the bridge" is a sentence fragment and cannot stand alone. No comma is necessary to join it with "He ran down the street." Note that this does not cover the use of "and" when separating items in a series, such as "red, white, and blue." In these cases a comma is not always necessary between the last two items in the series, but in general it is best to use one.

Parenthetical Expressions

Commas should separate parenthetical expressions such as the following: *after all*, *by the way*, *for example*, *in fact*, and *on the other hand.*

Example: *By the way, she is in my biology class.*

If the parenthetical expression is in the middle of the sentence, a comma is placed both before and after it.

Example: *She is, after all, in my biology class.*

However, these expressions are not always used parenthetically, so commas may not be necessary. To determine if an expression is parenthetical, see if you need to pause when you read the sentence. If you do, then it is parenthetical and needs commas.

Example: *You can tell by the way she plays the violin that she enjoys its music.*

No pause is necessary in reading that example sentence. Therefore, the phrase "by the way" does not need commas around it.

Hyphens

Hyphenate a **compound adjective** that is directly before the noun it describes.

Example 1: He was the best-known kid in the school.
Example 2: The shot came from that grass-covered hill.
Example 3: The well-drained fields were dry soon after the rain.

Use Your Ear

Read each sentence carefully, inserting the answer choices in the blanks. Don't stop at the first answer choice if you think it is right, but read them all. What may seem like the best choice at first may not be after you have had time to read all of the choices. Allow your ear to determine what **sounds right**. Often one or two answer choices can be immediately ruled out because they don't sound logical or make sense.

Contextual Clues

It bears repeating that contextual clues offer a lot of help in determining the best answer. Key words in the sentence will allow you to determine exactly which answer choice is the best replacement text.

Example:

Archeology has shown that some of the ruins of the ancient city of Babylon are approximately 500 years ________ Mesopotamian predecessors.

a. as old as any supposed
b. as old as their supposed
c. older than their supposed
d. older than a supposed

In this example, the **key word** "supposed" is used. Archaeology would either confirm that the predecessors to Babylon were more ancient or disprove that supposition. Since supposed was used, it would imply that archaeology had disproved the accepted belief, making Babylon actually older, not as old as, so either answer choice C or D is correct.

Since choice D contains the word "a," this would be correct if "predecessors" was singular. Since "predecessors" is plural (with an "s" on the end), choice C must be correct.

Furthermore, because "500 years" is used, answer choices A and B can be ruled out. Years are used to show either absolute or relative age. If two objects are as old as each other, no years are necessary to describe that relationship, and it would be sufficient to say, "The ancient city of Babylon is approximately as old as their supposed Mesopotamian predecessors," without using the term "500 years."

Simplicity is Best

Simplicity cannot be overstated. You should never choose a longer, more complicated, or wordier replacement if a simple one will do. When a point can be made with fewer words, choose that answer. However, do not sacrifice the flow of text for simplicity. If an answer is simple, but does not make sense, then it is not correct.

Beware of **added phrases** that don't add anything of meaning, such as "to be" or "as to them." Often these added phrases will occur just before a colon, which may indicate a list of items. However, the colon does not need a lengthy introduction.

The phrases "of which [...] are" in the below examples are wordy and unnecessary. They should be removed and the colon placed directly after the words "sport" and "following".

Example 1: *There are many advantages to running as a sport, of which the top advantages are:*

Example 2: *The school supplies necessary were the following, of which a few are:*

Don't Panic

Panicking will not put down any more words on paper. Therefore, it isn't helpful. When you first see the topic, if your mind goes blank, take a deep breath. Force yourself to mechanically go through the steps listed earlier.

Secondly, don't get clock fever. It's easy to be overwhelmed when you're looking at a page that is mostly blank, your mind is full of random, confused thoughts, and the clock is ticking down faster than you would like. But you brainstormed first so you don't have to keep coming up with ideas. If you're running out of time and you have a lot of ideas you haven't covered, don't be afraid to make some cuts. Start picking the best of the remaining ideas and expand on those few. Don't feel like you have to write down and expand all of your ideas.

Check Your Work

It is more important to have a shorter paper that is well written and well organized than a longer paper that is poorly written and poorly organized. Don't keep writing about a subject just to add words and sentences, and certainly don't start repeating yourself. Expand on the ideas that you identified in the brainstorming session and make sure that you save a few minutes at the end to review.

Leave time at the end, at least a few minutes, to go back and **check over your work**. Reread and make sure that everything you've written makes sense and flows well. Clean up any spelling or grammar mistakes that you might have made.

As you proofread, make sure there aren't any sentence fragments or run-ons. Check for sentences that are too short or too long. If the sentence is too short, check to see if you have an identifiable subject and verb. If it is too long, break it up into two separate sentences. Watch out for any "big" words you may have used. It's good to use difficult vocabulary words, but only if you are positive that you are using them correctly. Your paper has to be correct, but it doesn't have to be fancy. You're not trying to impress anyone with your vocabulary, but with your ability to develop and express ideas.

Summary

Depending on your test-taking preferences and personality, the writing will probably be your hardest or your easiest section. You are required to go through the entire process of writing a paper in a brief amount of time, which can be quite a challenge.

Focus on each of the steps listed above. Go through the process of creative flow first, generating ideas and thoughts about the topic. Then organize those ideas into a smooth, logical flow. Pick out the best ideas from your list. Decide which main idea or angle of the topic you will discuss.

Create a recognizable structure in your paper, with an introductory paragraph explaining what you have decided on and what your main points will be. Use the body paragraphs to expand on those main points and have a conclusion that wraps up the issue or topic.

Save a few moments to go back and review what you have written. Clean up any minor mistakes and give it those last few critical touches that can make a huge difference. Finally, be proud and confident of what you have written!

Speaking

In the speaking section, a topic will be presented to you and you must provide a short speech in response to the topic. Both the preparation and the speech must take place within the time allowed. There is not a correct answer to the topic. You must evaluate the topic, organize your ideas, and develop them into a cohesive and coherent response.

There are three speaking tasks, including retelling written and spoken input and speaking in a simulated interview.

You will be scored on how well you are able to utilize standard spoken English, organize and explain your thoughts, and speak clearly to address the question.

Of all the test sections on the TOEFL, this is the easiest to prepare for. This is the test section that you can practice anywhere, in your car, in your room, on the phone, by yourself, or with someone else. After you successfully pass TOEFL, you will be speaking English a lot, so you might as well prepare by speaking it at every opportunity beforehand.

Tips for the Speaking Section

The speaking section will require you to demonstrate your ability to speak English in both academic and informal settings. This involves speaking in an organized and clear manner without much preparation time. You will be asked to give four short speeches ranging from 45 to 60 seconds regarding a variety of topics.

Tip 1: Answering the Question

The speaking section of the test provides you with very little time to accomplish your goal of answering a question. Make sure that you spend your time saying things that matter and avoid saying things that do not. To practice, record yourself speaking about familiar topics. Go back and listen to yourself and identify unnecessary information. Try answering again until you think you have answered the question without digressing.

Tip 2: Speaking Clearly

A major part of speech requires you to pace yourself and speak not too quickly or too slowly. Speakers should also place adequate emphasis on key words, such as important nouns and verbs in each sentence. For practice, record yourself speaking or have someone listen to you and point out areas that are confusing.

Tip 3: Grammatical Accuracy

While speaking, grammatical accuracy plays a key point in clearly communicating what you mean. Try recording your responses to questions about familiar topics, and write down your answers or listen for grammatical errors. To help keep your grammar clear, make your points simple rather than complex.

Tip 4: Organization

Similar to the way writing should be organized with an introduction, three main points, and a conclusion, short speeches should be organized to make sure that everything that is said is to the point or supports the main objective. Practice making short arguments with clear points.

Tip 5: Using Time Effectively

Remember that the speaking section provides you with only 15 seconds to prepare and 45 seconds to answer the questions. Practice timing yourself answering questions and take note if you are speaking too quickly or including unnecessary information. Try practicing with a variety of topics.

Practice Tips:

- Make and practice a list of familiar topics and a few that you may not know much about.
- Verbally practice retelling specific days (yesterday, a holiday, etc.). Make sure to practice using prepositions and other connecting words, such as first, next, then, throughout.
- Practice telling short stories from your experiences in under a minute.
- Read or listen to a story and retell it.

Record yourself and ask yourself the following questions:

- Did I complete the task?
- Did I speak clearly?
- Did I make any grammatical errors?
- Were my points organized?
- Did I use my time well?

Preparing to Speak

Brainstorm

Spend your preparation time thinking of your main answer and a few points supporting your conclusion, as if this were a written response. Time is key, so do not try to think of too many reasons, but only what can be explained simply and clearly.

The Clear Message of a Speech

When speaking, you should be focusing on three fundamental **factors**: ideas, organization, and support. The most important thing for you to consider is whether the main ideas are *logical and clearly expressed*. If the ideas are comprehensible, you should then consider whether they have been expressed in the *logical order*, or whether you have presented them in a disorganized fashion. Finally, you need to consider whether your main ideas have been adequately *supported* by logic or facts. Do you provide enough support for your arguments to remain credible? Is the evidence provided relevant to the main ideas?

Exhausting the Possibilities

You will be prompted with some basic questions. There are only so many possible basic questions that can be asked about someone, so you can easily be prepared for every possibility. Go through and write down all the possibilities and a good answer for each. When you're asked about your family, you don't have to struggle to come up with descriptions for your family members. Practice ahead of time and know what you're going to say. Right now, as you're reading this, stop and take a minute to answer each of the following questions. If these were asked in an interview, what would you say?

1. Please describe yourself.
2. Please describe your family.
3. Please describe your home.
4. Please describe some of your interests.

5. Please describe your job.
6. Please describe your studies.

This is important practice. Make sure that you can spend a minute or so answering each of these questions without having to take time to think of a good response. These are basic questions and you should have your basic answers ready.

Tell a Story

Think about your favorite relatives. In many cases, they are your favorite because they are such raconteurs, or good storytellers. These are your aunts and uncles that can turn a simple trip to the grocery store into high adventure and keep you captivated and entertained. Even if you're not a natural storyteller, with a little thought and practice, even you can turn dull past experiences into exciting exploits.

Stories are your strongest weapon for demonstrating your mastery of speaking English. Some questions practically beg for stories to be told. These need to be compelling stories, real time drama, with you as the hero. Once you begin a quick, exciting story, you have set the tone.

The easiest way to prepare for these more difficult questions is to scour your memory for any exciting instance in your **past**, perhaps where you played a leadership role or accomplished a goal. This can be from any part of your past: during your education, at home with your family, doing a project at work, or anything that you might have had a part in. Identify the main characteristics of the story so you have the details correct. Make sure you know the basics of what happened, who was involved, why it occurred, and how the events unfolded sequentially. You certainly don't want to stumble over the facts and repeat yourself during your response.

One Size Fits All

These basic stories are building blocks. Just as a piece of lumber can be cut into many different shapes and have many completely unique uses, each of your stories does not only answer one unique question. Your stories are **one size fits all**. With practice you will find that you can use the same story to answer two seemingly unrelated questions.

For example, a question about teamwork and a question about working under pressure can both be answered by a story about your experience playing intramural basketball. The story could describe how you had to work as a team in order to get into the playoffs, spending time practicing together, coordinating plays, and whatever was necessary for the team to advance. Alternatively, the story could focus on the shots that you made that season in order to win the game in the last few seconds of play under enormous pressure. The basic story is the same: your experiences playing basketball.

The questions were different, but you **customized** the story to fit the question. With practice you should be able to answer almost any question with just a few stock stories that can be customized.

Find the Bridges

Some questions will lend themselves more readily to a story than others. You must have a set of basic stories ready that can be modified to fit the occasion. You must "find the bridges" in the questions offered to make sure your stories get told.

In WWII, the US Army used Bailey bridges. Bailey bridges were made of prefabricated steel sections that were carried around and could be thrown together at a moment's notice, allowing the army to move quickly across any obstacle and get to their destination.

You need to find bridges, i.e. **opportunities to tell your stories**. Look for any chance to turn a standard question about anything, into a bridge to begin telling your story. For example, "What is your job title?"

On the surface that might not seem like the ideal bridge, but with a little insight your response might become:

"My job title is Product Line Manager. I am responsible for everything from the development of new products to the obsolescence of old products. Marketing, sales, engineering, and production of the entire product line fall under my responsibility. One of the products was even my own idea based on feedback I received from my interactions with our customers. In the first year, it alone had achieved a sales level of over..."

The key to remember is that just because a question is **closed-ended** (yes/no or one word answers), you don't have to answer it as a closed-ended question. Answer the question asked, but then find a way to develop your answer into a bridge to a good story of yours. With an open mind, the most closed-ended of questions can become a launch pad into a story.

PRACTICE MAKES PERFECT

Don't try to answer every question spontaneously. You'll spend most of your time trying to think of what happened and repeating yourself. Beforehand, think of the classic stories you could tell and then **practice** going over them with your friends, explaining how you successfully achieved the goal or took charge and gave leadership to your group project. You don't want to have the story memorized, because it will become stale in the telling, but you want it to be smooth. This story must be live and in living color, so that a potential listener could see himself taking part and watching the situation unfold. Have your friends and family members quiz you by asking you random questions and see how well you can adapt to the question and give a clear response.

TOEFL Practice Test

Listening

This section will involve listening to a brief audio clip and then responding. To access the audio for this section of the test, please visit URL and enter the following six-digit code: 101067:
mometrix.com/academy/toefl-speaking-and-listening/

SCAN HERE

LISTEN AND REPLY PART 1

1. Listen to TOEFL Essentials Listening Q1 only one time. Choose the best response.

a. I prefer toast.
b. I haven't either.
c. In fifteen minutes.
d. Yes, we will have breakfast.

2. Listen to TOEFL Essentials Listening Q2 only one time. Choose the best response.

a. I heard the drinks are expensive.
b. Yes, I even bought a novel to read while I was there.
c. Everything here is very new.
d. My brother likes to buy books.

3. Listen to TOEFL Essentials Listening Q3 only one time. Choose the best response.

a. I have never been to a theater.
b. I should have worn a jacket.
c. I bought my ticket.
d. It was entertaining.

4. Listen to TOEFL Essentials Listening Q4 only one time. Choose the best response.

a. I'm sorry I'm late.
b. Straight ahead two blocks.
c. I don't have any cash.
d. On the international aisle.

5. Listen to TOEFL Essentials Listening Q5 only one time. Choose the best response.

a. Over the winter holiday.
b. Yes, I would like to go home.
c. I will take a train home.
d. I am living in an apartment.

6. Listen to TOEFL Essentials Listening Q6 only one time. Choose the best response.

a. I rode a bike to work today.
b. It's five blocks away.
c. I usually take the bus.
d. I can drive you home.

Listen to a Conversation Part 1

For the next two questions, listen to TOEFL Essentials Listening Q7-8 only one time.

7. Who most likely is the woman?

a. A librarian
b. A teacher
c. A salesman
d. A server

8. What did the man bring with him?

a. Their lunch
b. A beverage
c. A dessert
d. A side of fruit

For the next two questions, listen to TOEFL Essentials Listening Q9-10 only one time.

9. Who is the man seeing to fix his problem?

a. A doctor
b. A mechanic
c. A teacher
d. A barista

10. What does the man have planned for the afternoon?

a. Go to a job interview
b. Go to dinner with friends
c. Adjust the tires on his car
d. Go to work

For the next two questions, listen to TOEFL Essentials Listening Q11-12 only one time.

11. What is the purpose of this announcement?

a. To make a change to the course outline
b. To assign additional reading for the week
c. To explain the assignment for the day
d. To group students for an assignment

12. What will students do when they complete their quiz?

a. Wait for the paper to be graded
b. Remain seated
c. Work on the next reading assignment
d. Hand in their paper and leave

For the next two questions, listen to TOEFL Essentials Listening Q13-14 only one time.

13. What is the purpose of this announcement?

a. To tell students about a change in the syllabus
b. To tell students about the weekly quizzes
c. To remind students about their exam on Friday
d. To offer students extra credit for turning in their assignments before midnight

14. Where will students take the weekly quizzes?

a. They are given in person
b. They are posted to the university website
c. They are posted in an online portal
d. They are printed in the class textbook

For the next four questions, listen to TOEFL Essentials Listening Q15-18 only one time.

15. Why does the speaker mention growing foods?

a. To explain how it would change if Yellowstone erupted
b. To address modern food production around the world
c. To suggest how we should adapt to current climate changes
d. To provide a solution for Yellowstone's future eruptions

16. What will the speaker probably discuss next?

a. The best way to prepare for Yellowstone's eruption
b. How to grow food during climate change
c. Additional supervolcanoes in the United States
d. How to prevent climate change

17. What is the main topic of the lecture?

a. The impact of agriculture on the climate
b. How to best prepare for volcanic eruptions
c. Where to visit to see a volcano
d. Volcanoes in the United States and the potential impacts of an eruption

18. What does the speaker mean by saying "the eruption would be catastrophic in nearby areas"?

a. There would be a great amount of damage to surrounding areas
b. Nearby areas would not be impacted
c. There would be a severe global impact
d. There would be no changes in any areas

For the next four questions, listen to TOEFL Essentials Listening Q19-22 only one time.

19. What is the main topic of this lecture?

a. How factories impact people's movement
b. The process of manufacturing textiles
c. The overall impact of the Industrial Revolution
d. How steam powered machinery changed the economy

20. What impact did the Industrial Revolution have on the population?

a. The population gradually decreased
b. The population grew quickly
c. There were no changes in the population
d. The population grew very slowly

21. Based on this lecture, what was the Industrial Revolution?

a. A period of time when there was a growing focus on manufacturing
b. A turning point for human rights
c. A place where factories were located
d. A period of time in which families relocated to rural towns

22. Why does the speaker mention an increase in pay for most families?

a. The cost of factory machinery was expensive
b. Factories hired less workers to save money
c. Families needed to be able to pay for the goods that were being produced
d. It impacted the quality of life for many and supported a growth in the population

Listen and Reply Part 2

23. Listen to TOEFL Essentials Listening Q23 only one time. Choose the best response.

a. We booked first class flights.
b. I'll return next Wednesday.
c. We have a long layover.
d. I am excited to go on vacation.

24. Listen to TOEFL Essentials Listening Q24 only one time. Choose the best response.

a. I packed my lunch today.
b. I volunteer at the shelter on weekends.
c. I go every Monday.
d. I walk to school most days.

25. Listen to TOEFL Essentials Listening Q25 only one time. Choose the best response.

a. I brought plates.
b. How much would you like?
c. It is vanilla.
d. To celebrate her birthday.

26. Listen to TOEFL Essentials Listening Q26 only one time. Choose the best response.

a. My supervisor did.
b. I told the teacher.
c. My neighbor is coming.
d. What is the project about?

27. Listen to TOEFL Essentials Listening Q27 only one time. Choose the best response.

a. In about 20 minutes.
b. In the top drawer.
c. Do you need a pen?
d. I bought them from the market.

28. Listen to TOEFL Essentials Listening Q28 only one time. Choose the best response.

a. Maybe, I will have dinner later.
b. No, I am not sure where you left your backpack.
c. Yes, I understand the assignment.
d. Yes, did you?

Listen to a Conversation Part 2

For the next two questions, listen to TOEFL Essentials Listening Q29-30 only one time.

29. What is most likely the relationship between these speakers?

a. Teacher and student
b. Roommates
c. Co-workers
d. Friends

30. Where will the meeting take place?

a. Online
b. In a conference room
c. At an office
d. In the boardroom

For the next two questions, listen to TOEFL Essentials Listening Q31-32 only one time.

31. What is the man most likely trying to do?

a. Purchase a car
b. Rent an apartment
c. Apply for a job
d. Obtain a new passport

32. When will the man know if he was approved?

a. At the end of this month
b. At the beginning of next month
c. In two weeks
d. In two business days

For the next two questions, listen to TOEFL Essentials Listening Q33-34 only one time.

33. What does the speaker say about Matthew Lomberg?

a. He will be refereeing the game
b. He has a record of leg injuries
c. He will not be playing
d. He plays for the Western University Bobcats

34. What does the speaker mean by "we are hopeful we still have what it takes to come out victorious"?

a. He thinks the fans will have fun
b. He thinks the team can win without the starting quarterback
c. He hopes the weather is nice
d. He wants the Bobcats to win

For the next two questions, listen to TOEFL Essentials Listening Q35-36 only one time.

35. What do students have to do to get credit for attending the art show?

a. Take a photo of the art in the Fisher Student Union
b. Draw their own version of art they like
c. Bring in their ticket and a written reflection
d. Come to class next Friday

36. Why do the students need to go to the art show?

a. It is required
b. It will help them learn
c. They will enjoy it
d. The teacher will be there

Reading

Vocabulary

1. Select the word that is closest in meaning to the word <u>develop</u>.

a. Destroy
b. Evolve
c. Inundate
d. Applaud

2. Select the word that is closest in meaning to the word <u>prepare</u>.

a. Direct
b. Dispense
c. Assemble
d. Deconstruct

3. Select the word that is closest in meaning to the word <u>support.</u>

a. Assist
b. Oppose
c. Circumvent
d. Eliminate

4. Select the word that is closest in meaning to the word <u>accurate</u>.

a. Stoic
b. Careful
c. Wrong
d. Correct

5. Select the word that is closest in meaning to the word <u>evaluate.</u>

a. Ignore
b. Assess
c. Complain
d. Console

General Reading: Daily Life

Read the following email.

To: Giavanni Montour
From: management@computerwiz.com
Date: 4/3/2021
Subject: Job Offer

Giavanni,

We had a wonderful time getting to know you during your interview. We think you would be a great fit for the front desk clerk opening and would like to offer you a part-time position. We would need you to work Monday, Wednesday, and Friday mornings from 9am to 3 pm.

The starting pay is $13.50 per hour. Once you complete your probationary period of 8 weeks, your pay will increase to $15.00 per hour. Attached, you will find information about the dress code and code of conduct for all Computer Wiz employees. Please read over it and feel free to ask any questions you have.

If you are still interested and ready to accept this position, please email me back or call the store so we can schedule a meeting to get you started.

Thank you,
Catalina Rivera
Manager, Computer Wiz

6. How can Giavanni find more information about the dress code and code of conduct?

a. By calling the store
b. By opening the email attachment
c. By completing the probationary period
d. By replying to the email

7. On which of the following days will Giavanni work?

a. Tuesday
b. Thursday
c. Wednesday
d. Sunday

8. What position will Giavanni be filling?

a. Manager
b. Assistant Manager
c. Front Desk Clerk
d. Salesman

9. What does Giavanni need to do to accept the job?

a. Call the store or email Catalina
b. Read the code of conduct
c. Complete his probationary period
d. Come to the store on Monday, Wednesday, or Friday

Read the following newspaper advertisement.

Danny's Dog Walking Service - Safe, Affordable - Great reviews! - 15 years of experience - All breeds, all sizes - Starting at $10 per walk Call 954-382-7938 Danny Caplin

10. Who is Danny Caplin?

a. A math tutor
b. A dog walker
c. A house painter
d. A server

11. How many years of experience does Danny have?

a. 10
b. 954
c. 15
d. 2

Read the following restaurant sign.

Marianna's Café **Now Open!** Free 8 oz coffee with the purchase of a pastry. Expires January 31st Open Monday through Saturday, 7am to 7pm Mayfaire Town Centre 5673 Birchwood Dr, Unit 3B

12. On which of the following days in Marianna's Café not open?

a. Monday
b. Tuesday
c. Friday
d. Sunday

13. When can customers get free coffee with the purchase of a pastry?

a. On Sundays
b. Until January 31st
c. Only on weekdays
d. Only on weekends

Read the following email.

To: Ryan Smith
From: ticketing@wildcatshockey.com
Date: February 17th
Subject: Tickets

Dear Mr. Smith,

Thank you for purchasing 4 tickets to the Wildcats vs. Bears game at 7pm on March 1st. Your tickets are attached. You can print them or display them on your mobile device to gain entry to the game.

Parking is available in the garage attached to the rink. Event parking is $20. If you prefer public transit, the Blue Line stop 3 is directly across from the rink.

All ticket sales are final. To learn more about this policy or to upgrade your seats, please visit wildcatshockey.com. Please take a moment to familiarize yourself with our attached bag policy so that we can expedite our entry process while keeping everyone safe.

We'll see you in the Wildcat Den soon!

14. What can Mr. Smith do at wildcatshockey.com?

a. Display his tickets
b. Upgrade his seats
c. Purchase parking
d. Print his tickets

15. How many tickets did Mr. Smith buy?

a. 7
b. 1
c. 3
d. 4

16. If Mr. Smith drives himself to the game, how much will he pay to park at the rink?

a. $20
b. $7
c. $3
d. Parking is free

17. Which of the following is an attachment to the email?

a. Parking passes
b. The bag policy
c. Ticketing policies
d. A public transit map

Academic Reading: Tables

Read about opossums. Then select true, false, or not stated.

Characteristics	Adaptations	Interesting Fact
• Cat sized body • Thick gray and white fur • Long, hairless tails • Docile	• Opposable thumbs on their back feet • Keen sense of smell to make up for poor eyesight • Prehensile tails to help climb trees	• Opossums are the only marsupial native to North America

18. Opossums use their tails to help them climb trees.

a. True
b. False
c. Not Stated

19. Opossums have great eyesight.

a. True
b. False
c. Not Stated

20. Opossums have short life spans.

a. True
b. False
c. Not Stated

21. There are several marsupials native to North America.

a. True
b. False
c. Not Stated

Read about coffee. Then select true, false, or not stated.

History	How it was used	Interesting Fact
• 800s: Ethiopian farmer discovered his goat being highly energetic after eating coffee beans • 1400s: Coffee houses began opening • 1700s: Most Americans switched from tea to coffee due to English taxes • 800s: Coffee became the most traded commodity in the world	• Medicinally • To aid concentration • As a stimulant	• Brazil is the world's largest coffee producer

22. The majority of Americans drank tea instead of coffee in the 1700s.

a. True
b. False
c. Not Stated

23. Coffee was sometimes used as medicine.

a. True
b. False
c. Not Stated

24. The United States does not produce any coffee.

a. True
b. False
c. Not Stated

25. Ethiopia is the world's largest coffee producer.

a. True
b. False
c. Not Stated

Academic Reading: Passages

Read this passage.

Pluto

Pluto is a dwarf planet found just beyond Neptune. It was originally discovered in 1930 and was considered the ninth planet in our solar system; however, in 2006 it was determined that Pluto should not be considered a planet because it is not large enough to have orbital dominance in the area in which it is located. This means that Pluto's gravity is not strong enough to pull in smaller objects that surround it. It is very small, about half the width of the United States. While Pluto is small, there are five moons that orbit around it.

Pluto is visible from Earth with the use of a telescope. Its surface is covered in valleys, plains, craters, and mountains. Pluto has water ice on its surface, and it is believed that there is an ocean beneath that. It is named for the Roman god of the underworld. Pluto rotates slowly, making a day there last 153 hours. Its revolution period, how long it takes to go around the Sun, is the same as 248 Earth years.

26. When was Pluto discovered?

a. 2006
b. 1930
c. 153
d. 248

27. Which of the following is found on Pluto's surface?

a. Mountains
b. Moons
c. Oceans
d. Comets

28. Why is Pluto not considered a planet?

a. It is too large
b. It is covered in ice
c. It has too many moons
d. It is not large enough to have orbital dominance

29. How long does it take for Pluto to revolve around the Sun?

a. 365 days
b. 153 hours
c. 248 years
d. 24 hours

30. If someone wants to look at Pluto from Earth, what will they need?

a. Binoculars
b. A telescope
c. A satellite
d. Nothing, they can see it with their naked eye

31. What is Pluto named after?

a. A Roman god
b. The ocean beneath its surface
c. Its rotational period
d. One of its moons

Read the following passage:

Vincent van Gogh

Vincent van Gogh is one of the most well-known painters in world history, but this wasn't always the case. Van Gogh was born to an upper-middle class family in the Zundert, Netherlands in 1853. He was a serious child and struggled with feelings of unhappiness from a young age when his mother sent him to boarding school. He was able to express himself through his art, which his mother encouraged. Through his adolescence and adulthood, van Gogh experienced many psychotic episodes. He returned home and spent time painting before moving to Paris, France in 1886 to work on his art. During this time, his mental health declined. This led to an altercation in which he cut off part of his own ear.

Van Gogh was not considered successful during his lifetime. He was considered insane and eventually committed suicide in 1890 at age 37. Following his death, his style of art began to grow in popularity and people began looking at his work with reverence. His paintings have since become some of the most expensive pieces ever sold, namely the *Portrait of Dr. Paul Gachet* which sold for 83 million dollars in 1990. Other well-known pieces by Vincent van Gogh include *The Starry Night, The Potato Eaters, Irises, Sunflowers,* and his self-portrait. A large number of his pieces went missing during the Nazi Period and were stolen from exiled or murdered Jewish collectors. Some of these pieces have disappeared completely but some have resurfaced in museums or at auctions. Those interested in learning more about van Gogh and seeing his art in person can visit The Van Gogh Museum in Amsterdam.

32. Which of Vincent van Gogh's paintings sold for 83 million dollars?

a. The Potato Eaters
b. Portrait of Dr. Paul Gachet
c. The Starry Night
d. Sunflowers

33. Where was Vincent van Gogh born?

a. Paris, France
b. London, England
c. Amsterdam, Netherlands
d. Zundert, Netherlands

34. How did many pieces of Vincent van Gogh's art go missing?

a. They burned in a fire
b. Vincent van Gogh destroyed them
c. They were stolen
d. Vincent van Gogh misplaced them while moving

35. When did Vincent van Gogh become famous and well regarded?

a. After his death
b. During adulthood
c. During childhood
d. When he moved to Paris

36. In what year did Vincent van Gogh die?

a. 1890
b. 1853
c. 1886
d. 1990

Writing

BUILD A SENTENCE

Select the correct order of phrases to make an appropriate sentence.

1. Have you been to the grocery store this week?

I __________ __________ __________ __________.

1 = go
2 = on
3 = usually
4 = Fridays

a. 1, 2, 3, 4
b. 4, 3, 2, 1
c. 1, 3, 2, 4
d. 3, 1, 2, 4

2. What did Iliza say about dinner tonight?

She __________ __________ __________ __________

1 = meet us
2 = will
3 = the restaurant
4 = at

a. 1, 2, 3, 4
b. 2, 1, 4, 3
c. 4, 3, 2, 1
d. 3, 1, 4, 2

3. Did the lunch delivery come?

Yes, __________ __________ __________ __________.

1= in
2= put it
3= the lunchroom
4= I

a. 4, 2, 1, 3
b. 2, 1, 4, 3
c. 4, 3, 2, 1
d. 2, 3, 4, 1

4. Did Jessica come to the party on Saturday?

She ______ ______ ______ ______.

1= weekend shift
2= had
3= the
4= to work

a. 4, 2, 3, 1
b. 3, 1, 2, 4
c. 2, 4, 3, 1
d. 2, 3, 4, 1

5. Are you ready to walk to lunch?

Not yet. ______ ______ ______ ______.

1= this email
2= I need
3= to
4= finish

a. 4, 2, 3, 1
b. 3, 1, 2, 4
c. 2, 4, 3, 1
d. 2, 3, 4, 1

6. I can't wait to go on vacation next week.

Did you ______ ______ ______ ______?

1= plan
2= your
3= activities
4= all of

a. 1, 4, 2, 3
b. 3, 1, 2, 4
c. 1, 3, 2, 4
d. 2, 3, 4, 1

7. Do you want to get dinner later?

Yes, ______ ______ ______ ______?

1= we
2= should
3= where
4= go

a. 1, 4, 2, 3
b. 4, 2, 1, 3
c. 1, 3, 2, 4
d. 3, 2, 1, 4

8. Do you know where David is?

He ________________ ________________ ________________ ________________.

1= since last
2= week
3= has been
4= out of the office

a. 1, 4, 2, 3
b. 2, 1, 4, 3
c. 3, 4, 1, 2
d. 4, 2, 1, 3

9. Have you been to the new sushi restaurant?

No, it is too ________________ ________________ ________________ ________________.

1= my
2= apartment
3= from
4= far

a. 4, 3, 1, 2
b. 2, 1, 3, 4
c. 2, 4, 1, 3
d. 1, 2, 4, 3

10. What movie should we watch?

The ________________ ________________ ________________ ________________?

1= one
2= about
3= time travel
4= new

a. 1, 4, 2, 3
b. 2, 3, 4, 1
c. 4, 1, 2, 3
d. 2, 3, 4, 1

11. I made an appointment with my academic advisor.

Great. She should ________________ ________________ ________________ ________________.

1= to take
2= you need
3= know
4= which classes

a. 4, 1, 2, 3
b. 3, 4, 2, 1
c. 1, 3, 2, 4
d. 3, 1, 4, 2

12. My laptop isn't starting.

Did you __________ __________ __________ __________?

1= try
2= it
3= plugging
4= in

a. 2, 3, 1, 4
b. 2, 1, 3, 4
c. 1, 3, 2, 4
d. 1, 3, 4, 2

13. Can I borrow your pen?

Sure, __________ __________ __________ __________?

1= I'm
2= not
3= using
4= it

a. 3, 1, 2, 4
b. 1, 2, 3, 4
c. 1, 3, 2, 4
d. 2, 1, 3, 4

14. Do you have any plans this week?

Yes, __________ __________ __________ __________.

1= going
2= to the
3= beach
4= we are

a. 4, 1, 2, 3
b. 3, 2, 1, 4
c. 4, 2, 3, 1
d. 1, 2, 3, 4

15. Where are you headed?

I'm __________ __________ __________ __________.

1= post office
2= the
3= going
4= to

a. 1, 4, 2, 3
b. 3, 4, 2, 1
c. 1, 3, 2, 4
d. 2, 1, 4, 3

Write an Email

16. You recently attended a leadership seminar. The presenter, Maxine Earl, has written an email asking for your feedback on her presentation.

You liked:

- The visual presentation was very easy to read and understand
- You feel like what you learned will be helpful in your job

One problem:

- You had a hard time hearing from the back row

Write a response. Tell the presenter:

- What you liked
- What problem you had
- If you would attend another of her seminars in the future

Describe A Photo

17. You took the following photo. You will post it on your social media. Describe your photo for your social media friends. Write complete sentences. Write as much as you can.

Write for an Academic Discussion

18. Your professor is teaching a class on technology. Write a post responding to the professor's question. In your response, you should:

- Express and support your personal opinion
- Make a contribution to the discussion in your own words

An effective response will contain at least 100 words.

Professor	By definition, technology as a noun is any useful product that develops from scientific application. Technology has the power to change how humans function in their day-to-day life. Quite often, we think of phones, computers, and other electronic devices as the first examples; however, these are only a few and maybe not the most important examples. Technology can be tangible, like the examples I just mentioned, but they can also be intangible, like software. Before the next class, please answer this question: What do you feel is the most important piece of technology ever invented and why?
Student One	I feel antibiotics are the most important piece of technology. Before their invention, simple infections could lead to lifelong impacts, like vision or hearing loss, loss of limbs, or even death. Antibiotics provide a treatment for infections and allow the human population to remain healthy.
Student Two	The printing press has been the most influential piece of technology for humans. This allowed people to reproduce writing in mass quantities and share it with more people than they could have before; therefore, allowing ideas and information to spread more rapidly.

Speaking

This section will involve listening to a brief audio clip and then responding. To access the audio for this section of the test, please visit URL and enter the following six-digit code: 101067:
mometrix.com/academy/toefl-speaking-and-listening/

SCAN HERE

READ ALOUD

Refer to the following information for questions 1-6:

You meet your friend at a bookstore.

1. Listen to TOEFL Essentials Speaking Q1 Speaker 1 one time only. Then read the following response out loud one time only.

Yes, I had some time between classes to come pick them up.

2. Listen to TOEFL Essentials Speaking Q2 Speaker 1 one time only. Then read the following response out loud one time only.

No. They don't have the book for one of my classes in stock. I really need it before the class starts on Monday, but they said it could be weeks before they have it back in stock.

3. Listen to TOEFL Essentials Speaking Q3 Speaker 1 one time only. Then read the following response out loud one time only.

Economics 101 with Mr. Smith. I have heard he is strict, so I want to make sure I am doing my best in that class.

4. Listen to TOEFL Essentials Speaking Q4 Speaker 1 one time only. Then read the following response out loud one time only.

Yes, please! That would be awesome. I will return it to you as soon as the bookstore has a copy I can buy. Thank you so much.

5. Listen to TOEFL Essentials Speaking Q5 Speaker 1 one time only. Then read the following response out loud one time only.

Great. I can get there around 3:30 or 5:45. Which time works best for you?

6. Listen to TOEFL Essentials Speaking Q6 Speaker 1 one time only. Then read the following response out loud one time only.

That sounds great. I will see you then. Thanks again!

Listen and Repeat

Refer to the following information for questions 7-14:

You are preparing to take a test in your university math class. Listen to the speaker and repeat what she says. Repeat only once.

7. Listen to TOEFL Essentials Speaking Q7 one time only. Repeat what was spoken out loud one time only.

8. Listen to TOEFL Essentials Speaking Q8 one time only. Repeat what was spoken out loud one time only.

9. Listen to TOEFL Essentials Speaking Q9 one time only. Repeat what was spoken out loud one time only.

10. Listen to TOEFL Essentials Speaking Q10 one time only. Repeat what was spoken out loud one time only.

11. Listen to TOEFL Essentials Speaking Q11 one time only. Repeat what was spoken out loud one time only.

12. Listen to TOEFL Essentials Speaking Q12 one time only. Repeat what was spoken out loud one time only.

13. Listen to TOEFL Essentials Speaking Q13 one time only. Repeat what was spoken out loud one time only.

14. Listen to TOEFL Essentials Speaking Q14 one time only. Repeat what was spoken out loud one time only.

Virtual Interview

Refer to the following information for questions 15-19:

You are interested in participating in a student exchange program. A representative of the exchange program will ask you some questions.

15. Listen to TOEFL Essentials Speaking Q15 one time only. Please answer the interviewer's question.

16. Listen to TOEFL Essentials Speaking Q16 one time only. Please answer the interviewer's question.

17. Listen to TOEFL Essentials Speaking Q17 one time only. Please answer the interviewer's question.

18. Listen to TOEFL Essentials Speaking Q18 one time only. Please answer the interviewer's question.

19. Listen to TOEFL Essentials Speaking Q19 one time only. Please answer the interviewer's question.

Personal Video Statement

The final portion of the TOEFL Essentials test is an unscored section where you will record a Personal Video Statement. You will record yourself answering two questions in English with the goal of expressing your unique personality to institutions.

The first question will always be,

- "What would you like to tell people about yourself?"

The second question will require you to select one of two randomly generated topics and give your opinion or response.

The rules for responses are as follows:

- You will have 30 seconds to prepare and 2 minutes to respond.
- Responses should be at least 1 minute in length and no more than 2 minutes.
- You may record a response again if desired, but only the second recording will be saved.
- You will not be able to review your recordings before you submit.

Answer Key and Explanations

Listening

Listen and Reply Part 1

1. C: When will breakfast be served? "In 15 minutes" (choice C) best answers the question because it provides a specific time for when breakfast will be served. "I prefer toast" (choice A) indicates a preferred breakfast food, not a specific time for when breakfast will be served. "I haven't either" (choice B) does not align with the question asked, as it does not address a specific time for breakfast. "Yes, we will have breakfast" (choice D) indicates that breakfast will be served eventually, but it does not give a specific time.

2. B: Have you been to the new bookstore? "Yes, I even bought a novel to read while I was there" (choice B) confirms that you have been to the new bookstore and that you purchased a book. Bookstores are not a place to purchase drinks, making "I heard the drinks are expensive" (choice A) incorrect. "Everything here is very new" (choice C) does not confirm if you have been to the bookstore, just that there are many new things in the area. Sharing that your brother enjoys buying books (choice D) does not address whether you have been to the new bookstore.

3. D: What did you think of the play? By responding that the play was entertaining (choice D), you are expressing what you thought of the play. Saying you have never been to a theater (choice A) does not express your opinion of the play even though it mentions a theater. Saying that you "should have worn a jacket" (choice B) is not related to the play. "I bought my ticket" (choice C) says that you purchased your ticket to the play, but not what you thought of it.

4. B: Could you tell me which way the grocery store is? "Straight ahead two blocks" (choice B) provides directions to the grocery store. "I'm sorry I'm late" (choice A) and "I don't have any cash" (choice C) do not give any directions. "On the international aisle" (choice D) gives the location of an item within a grocery store but does give directions to the store.

5. A: When will you go back home to visit? "Over the winter holiday" (choice A) provides a time for when you will go home to visit. Saying that you would like to go home (choice B) does not provide a time for when you will go, it only expresses that you want to. Saying that you will take a train (choice C) tells how you will go home but not when. Saying that you live in an apartment (choice D) explains where you are living now, not when you will go home.

6. B: How far away is the train station? "It's five blocks away" (choice B) best answers this question because it provides the specific distance to the train station. Sharing that you rode your bike (choice A) or that you usually take the bus (choice C) describes how to make your commute but not the location of the train station. Offering a ride home (choice D) does not explain how far away the train station is.

Listen to a Conversation Part 1

7. D: Good morning, can I please take your order? Yes, I would like a chicken sandwich with a side of fruit. Okay, would you like anything to drink? No thank you, I brought my own. In this scenario, the woman is most likely a server working in a restaurant and is taking the man's order. A librarian (choice A) would be more likely to ask if the man needed help locating a book. Teachers (choice B) would ask questions related to learning. A salesman (choice C) would inquire about the man's needs and attempt to sell him a good or service.

8. B: Good morning, can I please take your order? Yes, I would like a chicken sandwich with a side of fruit. Okay, would you like anything to drink? No thank you, I brought my own. The man indicates they brought their own drink when asked if they would like to order one. In this scenario, it is likely that the man is ordering his lunch; therefore, he did not bring it with him (choice A). There is no indication of a dessert being ordered or brought (choice C). A side of fruit (choice D) was ordered with the sandwich, so it was not brought by the man.

9. B: The tires need to be rotated. How long does that take? We can have it done in about 30 minutes. Great, I have a job interview to get to this afternoon. A mechanic (choice B), someone who works on cars, is the most likely person to do work on tires. A doctor (choice A) would be more likely to ask medical questions. A teacher (choice C) would ask questions related to learning. A barista (choice D), someone who works in a café, would ask what kind of coffee the man wants.

10. A: The tires need to be rotated. How long does that take? We can have it done in about 30 minutes. Great, I have a job interview to get to this afternoon. At the end of the conversation, the man indicates he has a job interview that he needs to go to (choice A). There is no mention of getting dinner with friends (choice B) or going to work (choice D). The mechanic will be adjusting the tires on the car (choice C), not the man with the job interview.

11. C: Listen to an announcement in a university classroom. Good morning, please find your seat and take out a pencil. I will be passing out a quiz based on this week's reading. It is 20 questions long and consists of multiple choice and short answer questions. You may start as soon as you receive your paper. When you finish, please hand the paper in to me and then you are free to go. In this announcement, a teacher is explaining what the assignment will be for the day. They have explained the format of the quiz and what students should do when they are done. There are no changes being made (choice A) in the announcement nor is there any reading being assigned (choice B). Students are also not being grouped to work together (choice D).

12. D: Listen to an announcement in a university classroom. Good morning, please find your seat and take out a pencil. I will be passing out a quiz based on this week's reading. It is 20 questions long and consists of multiple choice and short answer questions. You may start as soon as you receive your paper. When you finish, please hand the paper in to me and then you are free to go. In the announcement, the teacher stated that students should hand in their paper once they have finished, and then they are free to go. This means they can leave class once they have submitted their work (choice D). The students should neither wait for their grade (choice A) nor stay in their seat (choice B) based on this announcement. They were not instructed to work on the next assignment (choice C).

13. B: Listen to an announcement in a university classroom. This class will have one quiz every week and will cover the assigned readings. You can find these quizzes in our online portal. Please submit them before midnight on Friday. The quizzes make up 20% of your grade, so it is important you do well on them. This announcement tells students about the assigned weekly quizzes (choice B). It explains where to find them and how important they are for students' grades. There is nothing mentioned about any changes to the syllabus (choice A). This announcement talks about quizzes that are happening every week, not an exam (choice C). The announcement mentions that the quizzes are due by midnight, but it does not offer extra credit (choice D).

14. C: Listen to an announcement in a university classroom. This class will have one quiz every week and will cover the assigned readings. You can find these quizzes in our online portal. Please submit them before midnight on Friday. The quizzes make up 20% of your

grade, so it is important you do well on them. The announcement says that weekly quizzes are posted in the class's online portal (choice C). The university website (choice B) is an online resource, but the quizzes are not posted there. The quizzes are online, not given in person (choice A) or printed in a textbook (choice D).

15. A: Listen to a lecture from a geology class. Within the United States, there are over 165 active volcanoes. Three of them are considered supervolcanoes, meaning they have erupted in the past with a Volcanic Explosivity Index of 8. The most well-known of these is Yellowstone Caldera, located in Yellowstone National Park in Wyoming. It last erupted around 70,000 years ago. If it were to erupt again, the impact would be widespread. Ashes and gases sent into the atmosphere from the eruption would cause changes in the climate. This would then lead to changes in the way humans live and function, particularly how and what types of food are grown and in what regions. While the eruption would be catastrophic in nearby areas, Yellowstone's eruption would not eliminate life globally. The likelihood of an eruption within the next several thousand years is minimal. In fact, it is likely it will never erupt again. The speaker explains that food production would change if Yellowstone erupted (choice A) because of the impact it would have on the climate globally. Because Yellowstone will not likely erupt again, this does not address modern food production (choice B) or what changes should be made at this time (choice C). While food production will likely change following an eruption, this lecture does not provide solutions for this (choice D).

16. C: Listen to a lecture from a geology class. Within the United States, there are over 165 active volcanoes. Three of them are considered supervolcanoes, meaning they have erupted in the past with a Volcanic Explosivity Index of 8. The most well-known of these is Yellowstone Caldera, located in Yellowstone National Park in Wyoming. It last erupted around 70,000 years ago. If it were to erupt again, the impact would be widespread. Ashes and gases sent into the atmosphere from the eruption would cause changes in the climate. This would then lead to changes in the way humans live and function, particularly how and what types of food are grown and in what regions. While the eruption would be catastrophic in nearby areas, Yellowstone's eruption would not eliminate life globally. The likelihood of an eruption within the next several thousand years is minimal. In fact, it is likely it will never erupt again. This lecture is focused on volcanoes, with a large focus on supervolcanoes. As such, it is likely the speaker will continue to talk about the rest of the supervolcanoes within the United States (choice C). Because the speaker mentioned that it is not likely there will be another eruption, they will probably not address how to prepare for such an event (choice A). The speaker mentions climate change as an effect of an eruption, but this lecture is not meant to focus on climate change (choices B and D).

17. D: Listen to a lecture from a geology class. Within the United States, there are over 165 active volcanoes. Three of them are considered supervolcanoes, meaning they have erupted in the past with a Volcanic Explosivity Index of 8. The most well-known of these is Yellowstone Caldera, located in Yellowstone National Park in Wyoming. It last erupted around 70,000 years ago. If it were to erupt again, the impact would be widespread. Ashes and gases sent into the atmosphere from the eruption would cause changes in the climate. This would then lead to changes in the way humans live and function, particularly how and what types of food are grown and in what regions. While the eruption would be catastrophic in nearby areas, Yellowstone's eruption would not eliminate life globally. The likelihood of an eruption within the next several thousand years is minimal. In fact, it is likely it will never erupt again. The main topic of this lecture is volcanoes, specifically the Yellowstone Caldera, and the potential impacts of an eruption (choice D). The lecture does not mention how agriculture impacts the climate (choice A), but instead mentions how a change in the climate after an eruption could impact agriculture. There is no mention of preparing for volcanic eruptions (choice B). There is mention of the location of the Yellowstone Caldera, but the location is not the main topic (choice C).

18. A: Listen to a lecture from a geology class. Within the United States, there are over 165 active volcanoes. Three of them are considered supervolcanoes, meaning they have erupted in the past with a Volcanic Explosivity Index of 8. The most well-known of these is Yellowstone Caldera, located in Yellowstone National Park in Wyoming. It last erupted around 70,000 years ago. If it were to erupt again, the impact would be widespread. Ashes and gases sent into the atmosphere from the eruption would cause changes in the climate. This would then lead to changes in the way humans live and function, particularly how and what types of food are grown and in what regions. While the eruption would be catastrophic in nearby areas, Yellowstone's eruption would not eliminate life globally. The likelihood of an eruption within the next several thousand years is minimal. In fact, it is likely it will never erupt again. By saying an eruption would be catastrophic in nearby areas, the speaker is saying that nearby areas would experience a great amount of damage (choice A). This is the opposite of there being no impact nearby (choice B). The speaker does mention global impacts but does not say they would be severe (choice C). There would be changes to the climate in both nearby areas and globally, so to say there would be no changes anywhere (choice D) would be untrue.

19. C: Listen to a history podcast. The Industrial Revolution shifted our society's focus from an agrarian society that focused on growing crops to a manufacturing economy that focused on the production of goods. This shift started in the mid-1700s in Great Britain and spread across Europe and to the United States. Factories began using machines to do tedious work that humans used to do by hand, and there was an increase in chemical manufacturing as well as a shift to water and steam powered machinery. Together, these things made the production of goods quicker and more cost efficient. To meet demands, many people began moving to cities from rural areas to work in factories. The pay from factory work led to an increase in the average household income, which then led to an improved quality of living for many families. Additionally, it meant families could financially support more children which led to unprecedented growth in the population. The growth in the manufacturing industry began to level off in the mid-1800s. This lecture explains what the Industrial Revolution was and how it impacted the economy, where people lived, and how that impacted the overall lifestyle of working families (choice C). While the lecture mentions that people moved into cities to work in factories (choice A), that is not the overall topic. Similarly, steam powered machinery (choice D) is mentioned, but it is not the main focus. The textile manufacturing process did change during the Industrial Revolution, but it is not directly mentioned in this lecture (choice B).

20. B: Listen to a history podcast. The Industrial Revolution shifted our society's focus from an agrarian society that focused on growing crops to a manufacturing economy that focused on the production of goods. This shift started in the mid-1700s in Great Britain and spread across Europe and to the United States. Factories began using machines to do tedious work that humans used to do by hand, and there was an increase in chemical manufacturing as well as a shift to water and steam powered machinery. Together, these things made the production of goods quicker and more cost efficient. To meet demands, many people began moving to cities from rural areas to work in factories. The pay from factory work led to an increase in the average household income, which then led to an improved quality of living for many families. Additionally, it meant families could financially support more children

which led to unprecedented growth in the population. The growth in the manufacturing industry began to level off in the mid-1800s. The lecture states that there was an unprecedented growth in the population. This means that it grew quickly in a way that it had not before (choice B). This is the opposite of slow growth (choice D) and means there was a significant change (choice C). There was not a decrease in the population (choice A).

21. A: Listen to a history podcast. The Industrial Revolution shifted our society's focus from an agrarian society that focused on growing crops to a manufacturing economy that focused on the production of goods. This shift started in the mid-1700s in Great Britain and spread across Europe and to the United States. Factories began using machines to do tedious work that humans used to do by hand, and there was an increase in chemical manufacturing as well as a shift to water and steam powered machinery. Together, these things made the production of goods quicker and more cost efficient. To meet demands, many people began moving to cities from rural areas to work in factories. The pay from factory work led to an increase in the average household income, which then led to an improved quality of living for many families. Additionally, it meant families could financially support more children which led to unprecedented growth in the population. The growth in the manufacturing industry began to level off in the mid-1800s. Based on this lecture, the Industrial Revolution was a time when society began to focus more on manufacturing goods than other types of production (choice A). There is no mention of human rights (choice B) in this lecture. The Industrial Revolution was a period of time, not a place where factories were located (choice C). Many families relocated from rural areas to cities, not the other way around (choice D).

22. D: Listen to a history podcast. The Industrial Revolution shifted our society's focus from an agrarian society that focused on growing crops to a manufacturing economy that focused on the production of goods. This shift started in the mid-1700s in Great Britain and spread across Europe and to the United States. Factories began using machines to do tedious work that humans used to do by hand, and there was an increase in chemical manufacturing as well as a shift to water and steam powered machinery. Together, these things made the production of goods quicker and more cost efficient. To meet demands, many people began moving to cities from rural areas to work in factories. The pay from factory work led to an increase in the average household income, which then led to an improved quality of living for many families. Additionally, it meant families could financially support more children which led to unprecedented growth in the population. The growth in the manufacturing industry began to level off in the mid-1800s. According to the lecture, the increase in pay from factory work directly impacted the quality of life for working families and lead to an increase in the population (choice D). Workers were not expected to pay for the factory machinery (choice A) nor were they required to buy the goods being produced (choice C). The lecture does not mention factories hiring less workers to save money (choice B).

Listen and Reply Part 2

23. B: When will you be back from your vacation? Saying that you will "return next Wednesday" (choice B) specifies what day you will come back from your vacation. Saying that you booked first class flights (choice A) describes how you will be traveling, but not when. Having a long layover (choice C) does not explain when you will be coming back, just that you will have to wait in the airport for a while between flights. Sharing that you are excited to go on vacation (choice D) does not answer when you will be returning, only that you are looking forward to going.

24. C: How often do you visit the library? By responding that you "go every Monday" (choice C), you are explaining that you go once a week on the same day. The question does not ask about meal choices, so saying you brought your lunch (choice A) is incorrect. Sharing that you volunteer at the shelter on the weekends (choice B) tells how often you volunteer, but not how often you visit the library. Saying that you walk to school most days (choice D) does not answer the question about visiting the library.

25. D: Why did Sydney bring cake today? By responding that the cake is to celebrate a birthday (choice D), you are explaining why Sydney brought cake today. Sharing that you brought plates (choice A) and that the cake is vanilla (choice C) does not specify why a cake was brought. Asking how much cake they would like (choice B) also does not give a reason for why the cake was brought.

26. A: Who approved the project? Saying "my supervisor did" (choice A) correctly specifies who approved the project. Saying that you told the teacher (choice B) does not indicate who approved the project. Similarly, saying that your neighbor (choice C) is coming also does not describe who approved the project. Asking what the project is about (choice D) does not explain who approved it.

27. B: Where are the staples? "In the top drawer" (choice A) describes exactly where to find the staples. "In about 20 minutes" (choice A) gives a time for something, not a location. Asking if they need a pen (choice C) does not help them find the staples. Sharing that you got the staples at the market (choice D) does not specify where they are now.

28. D: Did you turn in your assignment? "Yes, did you" (choice D) confirms that you did turn in the assignment and want to know if they did as well. "Maybe, I will have dinner later" (choice A) does not address the assignment, neither does "no, I am not sure where you left your backpack" (choice B). Saying that you understand the assignment (choice C) does not answer if you turned it in.

Listen to a Conversation Part 2

29. C: I am scheduling a meeting for tomorrow to discuss the upcoming changes to the events calendar. What time is the meeting? 10:30 am. Is it virtual or in person? It is virtual so that our entire team can make it. Thank you. I have some questions about the changes, so I am looking forward to it. This conversation is about changes to an event calendar and a meeting to discuss them, so it is most likely that these people are co-workers (choice C). A teacher and student (choice A) would be more likely to talk about assignments or what has been discussed in class. Roommates (choice B) and friends (choice D) would be more likely to have casual, friendly conversation and not discuss meetings and work assignments.

30. A: I am scheduling a meeting for tomorrow to discuss the upcoming changes to the events calendar. What time is the meeting? 10:30 am. Is it virtual or in person? It is virtual so that our entire team can make it. Thank you. I have some questions about the changes, so I am looking forward to it. Speaker One says that the meeting will be virtual, that means it will take place online (choice A). Because it is virtual, there is no physical location for the meeting, such as a conference room (choice B), office (choice C), or boardroom (choice D).

31. B: The application fee is $50. If you are approved, we will have a unit available for you to move into at the end of the month. Rent will be due at the start of every month. What kinds of documents do I need to apply? You will need your ID and proof of income. How long will it take to get approved? We usually process the application within two business days. The man is attempting to rent an apartment (choice B). This is evident from the mention of moving into a unit and the due date for rent. Purchasing a car (choice A) would not require rent every month.

There is an application mentioned in this conversation, but it is for renting an apartment not for a job (choice C). There is no mention of a passport in this conversation (choice D).

32. D: The application fee is $50. If you are approved, we will have a unit available for you to move into at the end of the month. Rent will be due at the start of every month. What kinds of documents do I need to apply? You will need your ID and proof of income. How long will it take to get approved? We usually process the application within two business days. Speaker One says that the application is usually processed in two business days (choice D). The end of the month (choice A) is when a unit will be available. The beginning of the month (choice B) is when the rent is due. There is no mention of anything happening in two weeks (choice C).

33. C: Listen to an announcement at a university sporting event. Hello everyone and welcome to Southern University's homecoming football game! We are very excited to have you here with us on this beautiful fall day. Since Southern University began hosting homecoming in 1953, we have only lost four homecoming games. One of those four losses was to the Western University Bobcats, who we are playing today. Even though our starting quarterback Matthew Lomberg is out with a lower body injury and will not be playing today, we are hopeful we still have what it takes to come out victorious. The announcer says that Matthew Lomberg has a lower body injury and will not be playing in today's game (choice C). The announcer does not mention the name of the referee (choice A), nor that Matthew has a record of sustaining leg injuries (choice B). The Western University Bobcats are the opponents for the game, not who Matthew plays for (choice D).

34. B: Listen to an announcement at a university sporting event. Hello everyone and welcome to Southern University's homecoming football game! We are very excited to have you here with us on this beautiful fall day. Since Southern University began hosting homecoming in 1953, we have only lost four homecoming games. One of those four losses was to the Western University Bobcats, who we are playing today. Even though our starting quarterback Matthew Lomberg is out with a lower body injury and will not be playing today, we are hopeful we still have what it takes to come out victorious. Saying "we are hopeful we still have what it takes to come out victorious" implies they think the team can win without the starting quarterback (choice B). The announcer does not mention the fans having fun (choice A). He does mention the weather (choice C), but it does not relate to the hope for victory. The Bobcats are the opposing team, so he would not want them to win (choice D).

35. C: Listen to an announcement in a university classroom. There is an art show taking place in the Fisher Student Union next week from Monday through Thursday. It is mandatory for all students in this class to attend. You must bring your ticket and a written reflection to class to get credit for attending. For your reflection, you should pick one piece of art on display and write about it. Make sure you include who the artist is, what medium they used to create it, and what you think it represents. These will be due next Friday when you come into class. In order to get credit for going to the art show, students need to bring in their ticket and a written reflection (choice C). The teacher does not ask them to take a photo of the art (choice A) or draw their own version (choice B). The ticket and written reflection are due in class next Friday, but coming to class does not mean they will get credit for going to the art show (choice D).

36. A: Listen to an announcement in a university classroom. There is an art show taking place in the Fisher Student Union next week from Monday through Thursday. It is mandatory for all students in this class to attend. You must bring your ticket and a written reflection to class to get credit for attending. For your reflection, you should pick one piece of art on display and write about it. Make sure you include who the artist is, what medium they used

to create it, and what you think it represents. These will be due next Friday when you come into class. In the announcement, the teacher says it is mandatory to attend the art show. This means it is required (choice A). The students may learn something (choice B) and they may enjoy it (choice C), but that is not why they need to go. The teacher does not mention that they will be there (choice D).

Reading

Vocabulary

1. B: Develop means to grow or advance something, which is closest in meaning to evolve (choice B). Destroy (choice A) has the opposite meaning, to break something down. Inundate (choice C) means to overwhelm. Applaud (choice D) means to approve of something in an enthusiastic way.

2. C: Prepare means to make something ready by putting things together. Assemble (choice C) is the word that is closest in meaning, as it means to put things together. Direct (choice A) means to manage a situation. Dispense (choice B) means to distribute something. Deconstruct (choice D) is the opposite of prepare and means to take something apart.

3. A: Support means to give assistance to or aid in some way. Assist (choice A) is the word that is closest in meaning, as it means to help. Oppose (choice B) means to disapprove of or resist. Circumvent (choice C) means to find a way around something. Eliminate (choice D) means to get rid of.

4. D: Accurate means that something is right or precise. Correct (choice D) has the same meaning. Wrong (choice C) has the opposite meaning, that something is incorrect or not right. Stoic (choice A) means not showing emotion. Careful (choice B) means to avoid danger or accidents.

5. B: Evaluate is closest in meaning to assess (choice B) because they both mean to judge the value or significance of an item or information. Ignore (choice A) means to pretend something does not exist or is not happening. Complain (choice C) means to express dissatisfaction. Console (choice D) means to offer comfort.

General Reading: Daily Life

6. B: The dress code and code of conduct were sent as an attachment to the email. Giavanni should call the store (choice A) or reply to the email (choice D) if he wants to accept the position. Completing the probationary period (choice C) will increase his pay after he starts the job.

7. C: The email states that the job is part time and Giavanni will need to work on Monday, Wednesday, and Friday. This means he will not work on Tuesday (choice A), Thursday (choice B), Saturday, or Sunday (choice D).

8. C: Giavanni was offered the front desk clerk position (choice C) in the second sentence of the first paragraph. This email was signed by the manager (choice A). Assistant manager (choice B) and salesman (choice D) positions are not mentioned in this email.

9. A: Catalina, the manager who sent the email, tells Giavanni to send her an email or call the store to accept the position (choice A). The code of conduct was sent as an email attachment and Giavanni should read it (choice B), but that is not how he will accept the position. He will have to complete his probationary period (choice C) after he accepts the job and begins working. Giavanni will work on Monday, Wednesday, and Friday (choice D) after he accepts the job.

10. B: Danny Caplin is a dog walker at Danny's Dog Walking Service (choice B). Tutoring (choice A), painting (choice B), and serving (choice D) are not mentioned in this advertisement.

11. C: The third bullet point in the ad says he has 15 years of experience (choice C). The cost of walks starts at $10 (choice A). 954 (choice B) is the area code for Danny's phone number. There is no mention of the number 2 (choice D) in this ad.

12. D. The advertisement says the café is open Monday through Saturday. This means the café is open Monday (choice A), Tuesday (choice B), Wednesday, Thursday, Friday (choice C), and Saturday, but it is closed on Sunday (choice D).

13. B: The advertisement says the offer for free coffee expires on January 31st (choice B), which means after January 31st customers will no longer get free coffee if they purchase a pastry. The café is closed on Sundays (choice A). The advertisement does not say that there are only certain days you can get free coffee (choice C) or that it only applies on weekends (choice D).

14. B: The third paragraph in the email says that he can read more about the final sales policy and upgrade his seats (choice B) at wildcatshockey.com. Printing (choice D) or displaying tickets (choice A) are mentioned in paragraph one. It says he must do one of these to gain entry to the game. Parking (choice C) is mentioned in paragraph two, but it does not discuss paying for parking.

15. D: The first sentence of the email thanks Mr. Smith for "purchasing 4 tickets" (choice D). The game starts at 7pm (choice A) on March 1st (choice B). The stop for public transit closest to the rink is number 3 (choice C).

16. A: According to the second paragraph, parking in the garage at the rink costs $20 (choice A); therefore, it is not free (choice D). The game begins at 7 (choice B). The number 3 (choice C) is the public transit stop across from the rink.

17. B: The last sentence in the third paragraph asks Mr. Smith to read over the "attached bag policy" (choice B). Parking is available but passes are not attached (choice A). Information about ticketing policies (choice C) can be found on their website according to the third paragraph. The email does not mention public transit maps (choice D).

Academic Reading: Tables

18. A: True. The third note under the "Adaptations" section says that opossums have "prehensile tails to help them climb trees."

19. B: False. The second note under the "Adaptations" section says that opossums use a "keen sense of smell to make up for poor eyesight."

20. C: Not Stated. The life span of opossums is not mentioned in any of the information in the table.

21. B: False. According to the "Interesting Facts" section, "opossums are the only marsupial native to North America"; therefore, there are no other marsupials in North America.

22. B: False. Under the "History" section, it states that most Americans switched from tea to coffee because of taxation.

23. A: True. Under the "Uses" section, it says coffee was used medicinally. This means it was used as medicine.

24. C: Not Stated. There is no mention of the United States producing their own coffee.

25. B: False. Under the "Interesting Fact" section, it says that Brazil is the world's largest coffee producer.

Academic Reading: Passages

26. B: Pluto was originally discovered and considered a planet in 1930 (choice B). In 2006 (choice A), it was decided it was a dwarf planet and recategorized. A day on Pluto lasts 153 Earth hours (choice C) while a year there is 248 Earth years (choice D).

27. A: On Pluto's surface, there are valleys, plains, craters, and mountains (choice A). Pluto is orbited by 5 moons (choice B), but they are not on the surface. The ocean (choice C) mentioned in the passage is beneath Pluto's surface, not on it. There are no comets (choice D) mentioned in this passage.

28. D: Pluto is not large enough to have orbital dominance (choice D), meaning it has a weaker gravity than other objects in the area. Pluto is not considered large (choice A). While Pluto is covered in ice (choice B) and does have many moons (choice C), these do not disqualify it as a planet.

29. C: It takes Pluto 248 Earth years (choice C) to fully revolve around the sun. It takes 153 hours (choice B) for Pluto to rotate on its own axis; this is the length of a day on Pluto. It takes the Earth 365 days (choice A) to revolve around the Sun and 24 hours (choice D) to rotate on its axis, but none of this is mentioned in the passage.

30. B: Pluto is only visible from Earth using a telescope (choice B), this means it is not visible with the naked eye (choice D). Binoculars (choice A) are not strong enough to be able to see Pluto and they are not mentioned in the passage. A satellite (choice C) is also not mentioned.

31. A: Pluto is named after the Roman god of the underworld (choice A). The passage does not mention the name of Pluto's ocean (choice B) or the names of its moons (choice D). The passage does give Pluto's rotational period (choice C), but it does not have a name.

32. B: The painting *Portrait of Dr. Paul Gachet* (choice B) was sold at auction for 83 million dollars in 1990. The Potato Eaters (choice A), The Starry Night (choice C), and Sunflowers (choice D) are all examples of well-known pieces of art by Vincent van Gogh, but they were not pieces that sold for 83 million dollars.

33. D: Van Gogh was born in Zundert, Netherlands (choice D) in 1853. He moved to Paris (choice A) as an adult to work with other artists. The museum that honors him and his art is in Amsterdam (choice C). London (choice B) is not mentioned in this passage.

34. C: Many pieces of Vincent van Gogh's art were stolen (choice C) from Jewish collectors during the Nazi Period. Van Gogh did not lose any belongings or art pieces in a fire (choice A). It is not known or mentioned in the passage if Vincent van Gogh destroyed his art (choice B) or lost any while moving (choice D).

35. A: Vincent van Gogh was considered insane and was not well respected as an artist until after his death in 1890 (choice A). During childhood (choice C), he was a quiet and sad child. During his adulthood (choice B), he struggled with declining mental health and psychosis which led to poor public opinion of him. This is also true of his time in Paris (choice D).

36. A: Vincent van Gogh committed suicide in 1890 (choice A). He was born in 1853 (choice B). He moved to Paris in 1886 (choice C). His painting *Portrait of Dr. Paul Gachet* was sold in 1990 (choice D).

Writing

Build a Sentence

1. D: "I usually go on Fridays" (choice D) is the proper way to arrange this sentence. This sentence has a subject, a verb, a preposition, and an object of the preposition. "I" is the subject of the sentence. The verb is "go"; "usually" is an adverb that precedes the verb. "On" is the preposition and the object of the preposition is "Fridays."

2. B: "She will meet us at the restaurant" is the proper was to arrange this sentence. This sentence has a subject, a verb, an object of the verb, a preposition, and an object of the preposition. "She" is the subject, this is followed by the adverb "will," the verb "meet," and the object of the verb, "us." "At" is the preposition with the object of the preposition being "the restaurant."

3. A: "Yes, I put it in the lunchroom" is the proper way to arrange this sentence. This sentence has an introductory phrase, a subject, a verb, an object of the verb, a preposition, and an object of the preposition. "Yes" is an introductory phrase and is separated from the rest of the sentence by a comma. "I" is the subject, "put" is the verb, and "it" is referring to the lunch order and is the object of the verb. "In" is the preposition while "the lunchroom" is the object of the preposition.

4. C: "She had to work the weekend shift" is the proper way to arrange this sentence. This sentence has a subject, an auxiliary verb, a verb, and an object of the verb. "She" is the subject of the sentence. "Had to" is an auxiliary verb, it helps to explain the main verb "work." "The weekend shift" is the object of the verb.

5. D: "I need to finish this email" is the proper way to arrange this sentence. This sentence has a subject, an auxiliary verb, a verb, and an object of the verb. "I" is the subject. "Need to" is the auxiliary verb that helps to explain the main verb "finish." The object of the verb is "this email."

6. A: "Did you plan all of your activities" is the proper way to arrange this sentence. This question can be answered with a yes or no, so it starts with a verb. The verb, "did," is followed by a subject, another verb, and the object of the verb. "You" is the subject, "plan" is the verb, and "all of your activities" is the object of the verb.

7. D: "Yes, where should we go" is the proper way to arrange this sentence. This sentence has an introductory phrase followed by an adverb, an auxiliary verb, a subject, and a verb. "Yes" introduces the sentence and answers the question that was asked. This is followed by the adverb "where" and the auxiliary verb "should." "We" is the subject of this sentence and "go" is the verb.

8. C: "He has been out of the office since last week" is the proper way to arrange this sentence. This sentence has a subject, an auxiliary verb, a verb, a subject of the verb, a conjunction, and a dependent clause. "He" is the subject, "has been" is the auxiliary verb, "out" is the verb, and "of the office" is the subject of the verb. "Since" is the preposition that joins the beginning of the sentence with the dependent clause "last week."

9. A: "No, it is too far from my apartment" is the proper way to arrange this sentence. This sentence has an introductory phrase followed by a subject, verb, adverb, adjective, a preposition, and an object of the preposition. "No" introduced the sentence and is followed by the subject "it." The subject is followed by the verb "is," the adverb "too," and the adjective "far." The preposition is "from" and the object of the preposition is "my apartment."

10. C: "The new one about time travel" is the proper way to arrange this sentence. This sentence has an article, an adjective, a subject, a preposition, and a noun. "The" is the article, and it is followed by the adjective "new" that describe the subject "one." "About" is the preposition that comes before the noun "time travel."

11. B: "She should know which classes you need to take" is the proper way to arrange this sentence. It has a subject, an auxiliary verb, a verb, and a dependent clause. "She" is the subject, followed by the auxiliary verb "should," and the verb "know." This is followed by a dependent clause "which classes you need to take."

12. D: "Did you try plugging it in" is the proper way to arrange this sentence. This question begins with a verb that is followed by a subject, two consecutive verbs, an object of the verb, and a preposition. "Did" is the verb that begins the sentence followed by the pronoun "you" that directs the question. "Try plugging" are two consecutive verbs followed by the object of the verb "it" and the preposition "in."

13. C: "Sure, I'm not using it" is the proper way to arrange this sentence. "Sure" is used to answer the question that was asked, this is followed by an independent clause made up of a subject, an adverb, a verb, and an object of the verb. "I'm" is the subject followed by the adverb "not" and the verb "using." "It" is the object of the verb.

14. A: "Yes, we are going to the beach" is the proper way to arrange this sentence. "Yes" is used to answer the question that was asked, this is followed by the independent clause made up of a subject, a linking verb, a verb, a preposition, and an object of the verb. "We" is the subject, "are" is the linking verb for the verb "going." The preposition "to" is followed by the object of the verb "the beach."

15. B: "I'm going to the post office" is the proper way to arrange this sentence. This sentence consists of a subject, a verb, a preposition, and an object of the preposition. "I'm" is the subject, "going" is the verb, "to" is the preposition, and "the post office" is the object of the preposition.

WRITE AN EMAIL

Sample Response One

Hello Maxine,

I am writing to provide feedback on the leadership seminar you presented last week. I really enjoyed the visual presentation you used. It was easy to read and understand. I feel like I learned a lot and will be able to use what I learned in my position at work.

On the way out, I mentioned to the venue manager that I couldn't hear very well from where I was seated in the back. She said they were working on installing a new sound system to fix that. If I could sit closer to the front or the sound system gets fixed, I would love to attend another seminar.

Sincerely,

Evelyn Burns

This email efficiently and successfully addresses all the required topics. There are no grammatical or spelling errors. The word choice is appropriate for the scenario.

Sample Response Two

> I attend your seminar and thought it was great! I didn't like that I couldn't hear from the back row, but I would attend another seminar if that was fixed.
>
> I think I should sit closer to the front next time. That way, I can hear and see you better. I hope this input helps with future seminar.
>
> Thank you,
>
> Evelyn Burns

This email has several errors. It lacks a proper greeting. The first line is written in present tense when it should be past tense, meaning it should say "I attended" not "I attend." Additionally, the last sentence in the body of the email says "I hope this helps with future seminar" but should say "seminars." The fact you enjoyed the visual presentation was not included in your response and the overall tone should be more formal.

Describe A Photo

Sample Response One

Yesterday, we kicked off our vacation in Queensland by riding some horse on the beach! I had a wonderful time. I ride the cream-colored horse in the middle here. They were very calm on our ride. As you can see, the beach is very beautiful. The sand is soft and the water is clear. It was a pretty sunny day, but it was a little chilly, so we wore our warmer clothes. Today we are going to brunch and then we will go snorkeling on this same beach.

This is a generally successful response, but there are some grammatical issues. In the first sentence of the first paragraph, it should say "horses" as it is plural instead of "horse" which is singular. In the following sentence, it should say "rode" in the past tense instead of "ride" in the present tense. Aside from that, this response is elaborate and detailed. It explains what the beach looks like, what the weather appears to be, and what the individuals pictured are wearing.

Sample Response Two

The bech is beautiful here!

We ride horse on bech today. The sun very bright and the water very clear.

We will snorkel here tomorrow.

This response has several errors with spelling and grammar. The word "bech" throughout should be "beach." The second and third sentences should say "We rode horses on the beach today. The sun was very bright and the water was very clear." The statements listed are loosely connected but do not form coherent enough statements to be considered a successful response.

Write for an Academic Discussion

Sample Response One

Internet is the greatest technology invention of all time. I like that I can talk to my friends on it and I can search up information when I am curious too. I use internet on my phone and on my laptop too. It is entertaining and also informative.

This response is not successful for this task. At first glance, it is far too short to answer the question thoroughly. It is written with an informative tone and should have an academic tone, as it is for a class.

Sample Response Two

The development of the internet has made a large impact on the way society functions, which is why I think it is the most important piece of technology. It allows quick and easy access to information from a variety of sources. It also provides many platforms for people across the globe to stay connected. Proper use of the internet and the resources it offers can give people what they need professionally and personally. Its continuous use by so many people supports my feeling that the internet is the most important piece of technology.

This response is successful for the task. It answers what the most important piece of technology is and provides information to support your opinion. There are no spelling or grammatical errors. This response is written in an academic tone and fits length requirements.

Speaking

Read Aloud

1. Yes, I had some time between classes to come pick them up. Listen to TOEFL Essentials Speaking Q1 Speaker 2 as an example of a correct pronunciation.

2. No. They don't have the book for one of my classes in stock. I really need it before the class starts on Monday, but they said it could be weeks before they have it back in stock. Listen to TOEFL Essentials Speaking Q2 Speaker 2 as an example of a correct pronunciation.

3. Economics 101 with Mr. Smith. I have heard he is strict, so I want to make sure I am doing my best in that class. Listen to TOEFL Essentials Speaking Q3 Speaker 2 as an example of a correct pronunciation.

4. Yes, please! That would be awesome. I will return it to you as soon as the bookstore has a copy I can buy. Thank you so much. Listen to TOEFL Essentials Speaking Q4 Speaker 2 as an example of a correct pronunciation.

5. Great. I can get there around 3:30 or 5:45. Which time works best for you? Listen to TOEFL Essentials Speaking Q5 Speaker 2 as an example of a correct pronunciation.

6. That sounds great. I will see you then. Thanks again! Listen to TOEFL Essentials Speaking Q6 Speaker 2 as an example of a correct pronunciation.

LISTEN AND REPEAT

7. Welcome back to class everyone! Listen to TOEFL Essentials Speaking Q7 again to practice your pronunciation.

8. Today, we will be taking our first exam of the semester. Listen to TOEFL Essentials Speaking Q8 again to practice your pronunciation.

9. This test will cover everything we have learned so far. Listen to TOEFL Essentials Speaking Q9 again to practice your pronunciation.

10. You are allowed to use your calculator for all of the questions. Listen to TOEFL Essentials Speaking Q10 again to practice your pronunciation.

11. I will give you scrap paper for you to work problems out on. Listen to TOEFL Essentials Speaking Q11 again to practice your pronunciation.

12. If you need more during the test, just let me know. Listen to TOEFL Essentials Speaking Q12 again to practice your pronunciation.

13. Are there any questions? Listen to TOEFL Essentials Speaking Q13 again to practice your pronunciation.

14. You may begin. Listen to TOEFL Essentials Speaking Q14 again to practice your pronunciation.

VIRTUAL INTERVIEW

15. What has inspired you to participate in this program? Do you have any experience living abroad?

Sample Response One

I have always wanted to experience living abroad and I think this is a great way to get that experience. One of my friends participated in this program and she said she really enjoyed it. I have never had the opportunity to live anywhere but my home country.

This is a sufficient response. It addresses both parts of the interviewer's question while explaining their interest in the program.

Sample Response Two

My family moved a lot when I was younger. We have lived in France, Sweden, the United States, and Mexico. I have only lived abroad with family, never by myself.

This response addresses only the question "do you have any experience living abroad," not why they want to participate in the program. In order to give the best response, the speaker should say why they want to participate in an exchange program.

16. What are you looking for in a host family? Are there any considerations we should know about or any requests you have?

Sample Response One

Ideally, I would love to live with a family hosting other students. I think it would be a great support system. Aside from that, there is nothing I can think of that would be important to me.

This is a successful response. It answers all parts of the question and there are no grammatical errors.

Sample Response Two

Any style of host family would be okay with me. I would need to live with a family with no pets. I have allergy.

This is a clear, concise response that answers the question and explains the speakers request. The final sentence should say "allergies," but the rest of the sentence is appropriate.

17. What countries are you most interested in visiting? Is there anywhere you would prefer not to go? Why or why not?

Sample Response One

I would like to live anywhere coastal, especially Australia or Greece! I am open to anywhere that is not too cold because I do not want to purchase winter gear.

The speaker explains what countries they would prefer, where they would not like to visit, and why they would not like to visit there. This response addresses all parts of the question. There are no grammatical errors.

Sample Response Two

I like mountains. I think they are beautiful and I enjoy hiking. I also think that the lifestyle in mountain areas suits me best.

While this response is a thoughtful explanation of why the speaker wants to live in a mountainous region, it does not tell what country they would like to visit. It also does not describe if there is any destination they would prefer not to go. This response is not successful.

18. How do you think this experience will impact your life? What would you look forward to the most?

Sample Response One

I have no travel before, so I think I will learn a lot. I want to make friend when I travel.

There are several grammatical issues with this response. It should say "I have not traveled before, so I think I will learn a lot. I want to make friends when I travel." This response does not provide much detail about how the speaker thinks their life will be impacted.

Sample Response Two

I think I will gain a new sense of independence being abroad without my family. I also think it would help me with my major, international business. The thing I would look forward to the most would be making new friends and being immersed in a different culture.

The speaker's response is satisfactory. It addresses all portions of the question with no grammatical errors.

19. Is there anything else you want us to know about you?

Sample Response One

Yes, I am currently taking Spanish classes and working on my fluency. I would like to be placed in a country that speaks Spanish so I can practice more. I speak English and German fluently. I would prefer to be placed in a country that speaks one of those languages if a Spanish speaking country is not an option.

This response explains in great detail something that is important to the speaker about their placement. There are no grammatical errors.

Sample Response Two

Yeah, I think I would thrive in this program. I enjoy experience new things and new people. I find it very fulfilling to learn by being immersed in something new.

This response starts with a casual tone, but it answers the question successfully. It addresses the question thoroughly with only one grammatical error. The word "experience" in the second sentence should be "experiencing."

Image Credits

licensed under CC BY-SA 4.0 (creativecommons.org/licenses/by-sa/4.0/)

Recreational horse riding on Noosa North Shore beach, Queensland, January 2019 by Kgbo.

(https://commons.wikimedia.org/wiki/File:Recreational_horse_riding_on_Noosa_North_Shore_beach,_Queensland,_January_2019,_01.jpg)

Common English Language Idioms

- **A blessing in disguise** – a situation which at first seems bad, but which turns out to be a good thing.
- "That red light was a blessing in disguise! If I hadn't stopped when I did, I would have been hit by another car."
- **A dime a dozen** – used when referring to something that is very common.
- "The watch I have is really a dime in a dozen. I really want one that is unique!"
- **Beat around the bush** – to avoid talking about the main topic (usually one which is uncomfortable).
- "Stop beating around the bush and just go tell her you like her."
- **Bite the bullet** – to face a problem or situation immediately rather than avoiding it.
- "I want to ask for two weeks off from work but I am afraid to ask my boss. I guess I should just bite the bullet and ask her."
- **Break a leg** – said as a replacement for telling someone good luck.
- "You'll do great at your performance. Break a leg!"
- **Call it a day** – to stop working for the day.
- "I've made a lot of progress and I'm tired. I'm going to call it a day."
- Can't make heads or tails of something – to not be able to understand something.
- "I've read the example in the textbook three times and I still can't make heads or tails of it."
- **Couch potato** – a lazy person.
- "You should stop being such a couch potato and go outside sometime."
- **Cut somebody some slack** – to allow someone to do something without judgment or hindrance.
- "Cut him some slack! He worked all week and needs some time to relax."
- **Cutting corners** – to only do a job partially or to skip steps in the process.
- "If you want to make good grades, you need to do the work thoroughly and not cut corners."
- **Don't count your chickens until (before) they hatch (they've hatched)** – to consider a payment or positive outcome as being yours before in possession.
- "Don't buy something that expensive just because you think you'll be paid next month. You shouldn't count your chickens before they've hatched!"
- **Drag one's feet** – to delay doing something unpleasant.
- "You should really go to the dentist for that toothache as soon as possible. Don't drag your feet!"
- **Egghead** – someone who is very intelligent.
- "He makes straight As in all of his classes without even studying! What an egghead."
- **Elbow grease** – hard work or a high degree of effort (usually manual labor).
- "Most household fixes don't need special tools; just a screwdriver and a little elbow grease will do it."
- **Easy does it** – a caution to be gentle or careful while performing a task.
- "Set it down slowly. I don't want the piano damaged from moving it. Easy does it."
- **Feeling blue** – to be sad.
- "Why are you sitting in the corner?"
- "I'm just feeling a little blue today."
- **Fit as a fiddle** – to be healthy.
- "I was sick for a couple of weeks, but now I'm as fit as a fiddle!"

- **Get something out of your system** – to do something so that you will not want or have to do it later.
- "I really was feeling sad, so I cried for a while to get it out of my system."
- **Get your act together** – to recognize that the previous action was not good enough and try to do better.
- "I've been skipping my reading every night and starting a bad habit. I need to get my act together starting today!"
- **Give someone the benefit of the doubt** – to trust someone without having a reason to do so.
- "He wanted to borrow my truck, but I've never seen him drive. Maybe I should give him the benefit of the doubt and let him have it anyway."
- **Go back to the drawing board** – to have a failed first attempt and try to start over.
- "Well, we tried and did not succeed. Time to go back to the drawing board."
- **Hang in there** – to persevere in a difficult or painful situation.
- "Your job has been really hard lately, but you've done well to hang in there!"
- **Hit the sack** – to go to bed (usually early).
- "I worked so hard today and am exhausted. I think I'll go ahead and hit the sack."
- **In over one's head** – to be in a situation that is too difficult to handle.
- "I'm in a calculus class and don't understand anything. I think I'm in over my head."
- **It takes two to tango** – to state that it is more than one person's responsibility or fault (usually said in a negative way).
- "She and I always fight about our relationship, but it's not all her fault. It takes two to tango."
- **It's not rocket science** – said about a relatively easy or simple task.
- "You just have to water the flowers occasionally. It's not rocket science."
- **Jump the gun** – to rush or do something too early.
- "I just couldn't wait! I jumped the gun and asked her to marry me last night."
- **Jump to a conclusion** – to make a judgment without hearing all of the evidence.
- "She thinks I'm rich because she saw me wearing a suit and driving a nice rental car. If she saw what I normally drive, she wouldn't have jumped to that conclusion."
- **Just kidding** – something said to indicate that the previous statement was not true and was meant as a joke.
- "She told me that she broke my phone, but then pulled it out and said 'just kidding!'"
- **Kill two birds with one stone** – to take care of two or more problems with one solution.
- "We need to get a new phone and clothes, so let's just go to the mall later and kill two birds with one stone."
- **Let someone off the hook** – to no longer hold someone to doing something they had agreed to.
- "My flight got cancelled, so you are off the hook for taking me to the airport."
- **Make a long story short** – to shorten or skip telling a story to reach the main point.
- "To make a long story short, we had a really good time in our trip to London."
- **No pain, no gain** – said to indicate that doing something can be hard or even painful, but that it indicates progress.
- "Running is so hard, but I have to do it. No pain, no gain."
- **On the ball** – to be ready or aware of what is happening.
- "He always has the reading done ahead of the time. He's really on the ball."
- **Pull someone's leg** – used to indicate joking.
- "I was pulling Susan's leg when I said I won the lottery."
- **Pull yourself together** – said to someone who is visibly emotional in an embarrassing way.

- "You look like an emotional wreck! Pull yourself together."
- **Quick study** - used to describe someone who learns quickly.
- "Everything comes so easily to Jim. He is such a quick study."
- **Rain or shine** - used to indicate that an event will happen no matter what happens. This does not necessarily apply to weather.
- "We are going to watch that new movie on Friday, rain or shine!"
- **Rub the wrong way** - used to indicate that an action or person is irritating.
- "He never seems like he is telling the truth and it really rubs me the wrong way."
- **So far, so good** - the work done up until this point has been done well.
- "I'm halfway done with building my house and so far, so good."
- **Speak of the devil** - said when talking about a person and they show up. Can be positive or negative.
- "Jim is such a nice guy!" (Jim then walks in) "Speak of the devil."
- **That's the last straw** - used to indicate that one too many bad things have happened.
- "My boyfriend spilled coffee on me and constantly says mean things. The last straw, though, was when he broke my phone! I'm going to break up with him."
- **The best of both worlds** - to have the benefits of two situations that usually don't co-exist.
- "She lives far enough away from the city that she can see the stars, but close enough to have a short commute. She really has the best of both worlds."
- **Time flies when you're having fun** - said when time seems to be going faster than normal while enjoying oneself.
- "Our day at the theme park went by too quickly! Time flies when you're having fun."
- **To make matters worse** - usually used last in a list of bad experiences.
- "I had a bad day. I stepped on a nail, ran out of gas, and to make matters worse, I still have to work tonight."
- **Under the weather** - used to say that someone is sick.
- "I can't come to the party tonight; I'm under the weather. "
- **Vice versa** - used to indicate a reversal of two things in the previous statement.
- "You earn money and then you can spend it, not vice versa."
- **We'll cross that bridge when we come to it** - putting off an issue for later.
- "We somehow got the car to start this time, but we will have to fix it at some point. We will cross that bridge when we come to it."
- **Wrap your head around something** - to try to understand.
- "Hey Jim, can you come and look at this?"
- "Not right now, I'm trying to wrap my head around something."
- **You can say that again** - a statement used to indicate agreement to someone else's statement.
- "I can't wait for payday."
- "You can say that again!"
- **Your guess is as good as mine** - used to indicate a lack of knowledge.
- "Hey, do you know which way it is to Peter's house?"
- "Your guess is as good as mine!"
- **Zip your lip** - said to tell someone to be quiet.
- "Hey! Zip your lip, the professor is talking."

How to Overcome Test Anxiety

Just the thought of taking a test is enough to make most people a little nervous. A test is an important event that can have a long-term impact on your future, so it's important to take it seriously and it's natural to feel anxious about performing well. But just because anxiety is normal, that doesn't mean that it's helpful in test taking, or that you should simply accept it as part of your life. Anxiety can have a variety of effects. These effects can be mild, like making you feel slightly nervous, or severe, like blocking your ability to focus or remember even a simple detail.

If you experience test anxiety—whether severe or mild—it's important to know how to beat it. To discover this, first you need to understand what causes test anxiety.

Causes of Test Anxiety

While we often think of anxiety as an uncontrollable emotional state, it can actually be caused by simple, practical things. One of the most common causes of test anxiety is that a person does not feel adequately prepared for their test. This feeling can be the result of many different issues such as poor study habits or lack of organization, but the most common culprit is time management. Starting to study too late, failing to organize your study time to cover all of the material, or being distracted while you study will mean that you're not well prepared for the test. This may lead to cramming the night before, which will cause you to be physically and mentally exhausted for the test. Poor time management also contributes to feelings of stress, fear, and hopelessness as you realize you are not well prepared but don't know what to do about it.

Other times, test anxiety is not related to your preparation for the test but comes from unresolved fear. This may be a past failure on a test, or poor performance on tests in general. It may come from comparing yourself to others who seem to be performing better or from the stress of living up to expectations. Anxiety may be driven by fears of the future—how failure on this test would affect your educational and career goals. These fears are often completely irrational, but they can still negatively impact your test performance.

Elements of Test Anxiety

As mentioned earlier, test anxiety is considered to be an emotional state, but it has physical and mental components as well. Sometimes you may not even realize that you are suffering from test anxiety until you notice the physical symptoms. These can include trembling hands, rapid heartbeat, sweating, nausea, and tense muscles. Extreme anxiety may lead to fainting or vomiting. Obviously, any of these symptoms can have a negative impact on testing. It is important to recognize them as soon as they begin to occur so that you can address the problem before it damages your performance.

The mental components of test anxiety include trouble focusing and inability to remember learned information. During a test, your mind is on high alert, which can help you recall information and stay focused for an extended period of time. However, anxiety interferes with your mind's natural processes, causing you to blank out, even on the questions you know well. The strain of testing during anxiety makes it difficult to stay focused, especially on a test that may take several hours. Extreme anxiety can take a huge mental toll, making it difficult not only to recall test information but even to understand the test questions or pull your thoughts together.

Effects of Test Anxiety

Test anxiety is like a disease—if left untreated, it will get progressively worse. Anxiety leads to poor performance, and this reinforces the feelings of fear and failure, which in turn lead to poor performances on subsequent tests. It can grow from a mild nervousness to a crippling condition. If allowed to progress, test anxiety can have a big impact on your schooling, and consequently on your future.

Test anxiety can spread to other parts of your life. Anxiety on tests can become anxiety in any stressful situation, and blanking on a test can turn into panicking in a job situation. But fortunately, you don't have to let anxiety rule your testing and determine your grades. There are a number of relatively simple steps you can take to move past anxiety and function normally on a test and in the rest of life.

Physical Steps for Beating Test Anxiety

While test anxiety is a serious problem, the good news is that it can be overcome. It doesn't have to control your ability to think and remember information. While it may take time, you can begin taking steps today to beat anxiety.

Just as your first hint that you may be struggling with anxiety comes from the physical symptoms, the first step to treating it is also physical. Rest is crucial for having a clear, strong mind. If you are tired, it is much easier to give in to anxiety. But if you establish good sleep habits, your body and mind will be ready to perform optimally, without the strain of exhaustion. Additionally, sleeping well helps you to retain information better, so you're more likely to recall the answers when you see the test questions.

Getting good sleep means more than going to bed on time. It's important to allow your brain time to relax. Take study breaks from time to time so it doesn't get overworked, and don't study right before bed. Take time to rest your mind before trying to rest your body, or you may find it difficult to fall asleep.

Along with sleep, other aspects of physical health are important in preparing for a test. Good nutrition is vital for good brain function. Sugary foods and drinks may give a burst of energy but this burst is followed by a crash, both physically and emotionally. Instead, fuel your body with protein and vitamin-rich foods.

Also, drink plenty of water. Dehydration can lead to headaches and exhaustion, especially if your brain is already under stress from the rigors of the test. Particularly if your test is a long one, drink water during the breaks. And if possible, take an energy-boosting snack to eat between sections.

Along with sleep and diet, a third important part of physical health is exercise. Maintaining a steady workout schedule is helpful, but even taking 5-minute study breaks to walk can help get your blood pumping faster and clear your head. Exercise also releases endorphins, which contribute to a positive feeling and can help combat test anxiety.

When you nurture your physical health, you are also contributing to your mental health. If your body is healthy, your mind is much more likely to be healthy as well. So take time to rest, nourish your body with healthy food and water, and get moving as much as possible. Taking these physical steps will make you stronger and more able to take the mental steps necessary to overcome test anxiety.

Mental Steps for Beating Test Anxiety

Working on the mental side of test anxiety can be more challenging, but as with the physical side, there are clear steps you can take to overcome it. As mentioned earlier, test anxiety often stems from lack of preparation, so the obvious solution is to prepare for the test. Effective studying may be the most important weapon you have for beating test anxiety, but you can and should employ several other mental tools to combat fear.

First, boost your confidence by reminding yourself of past success—tests or projects that you aced. If you're putting as much effort into preparing for this test as you did for those, there's no reason you should expect to fail here. Work hard to prepare; then trust your preparation.

Second, surround yourself with encouraging people. It can be helpful to find a study group, but be sure that the people you're around will encourage a positive attitude. If you spend time with others who are anxious or cynical, this will only contribute to your own anxiety. Look for others who are motivated to study hard from a desire to succeed, not from a fear of failure.

Third, reward yourself. A test is physically and mentally tiring, even without anxiety, and it can be helpful to have something to look forward to. Plan an activity following the test, regardless of the outcome, such as going to a movie or getting ice cream.

When you are taking the test, if you find yourself beginning to feel anxious, remind yourself that you know the material. Visualize successfully completing the test. Then take a few deep, relaxing breaths and return to it. Work through the questions carefully but with confidence, knowing that you are capable of succeeding.

Developing a healthy mental approach to test taking will also aid in other areas of life. Test anxiety affects more than just the actual test—it can be damaging to your mental health and even contribute to depression. It's important to beat test anxiety before it becomes a problem for more than testing.

Study Strategy

Being prepared for the test is necessary to combat anxiety, but what does being prepared look like? You may study for hours on end and still not feel prepared. What you need is a strategy for test prep. The next few pages outline our recommended steps to help you plan out and conquer the challenge of preparation.

Step 1: Scope Out the Test

Learn everything you can about the format (multiple choice, essay, etc.) and what will be on the test. Gather any study materials, course outlines, or sample exams that may be available. Not only will this help you to prepare, but knowing what to expect can help to alleviate test anxiety.

Step 2: Map Out the Material

Look through the textbook or study guide and make note of how many chapters or sections it has. Then divide these over the time you have. For example, if a book has 15 chapters and you have five days to study, you need to cover three chapters each day. Even better, if you have the time, leave an extra day at the end for overall review after you have gone through the material in depth.

If time is limited, you may need to prioritize the material. Look through it and make note of which sections you think you already have a good grasp on, and which need review. While you are studying, skim quickly through the familiar sections and take more time on the challenging parts.

Write out your plan so you don't get lost as you go. Having a written plan also helps you feel more in control of the study, so anxiety is less likely to arise from feeling overwhelmed at the amount to cover.

Step 3: Gather Your Tools

Decide what study method works best for you. Do you prefer to highlight in the book as you study and then go back over the highlighted portions? Or do you type out notes of the important information? Or is it helpful to make flashcards that you can carry with you? Assemble the pens, index cards, highlighters, post-it notes, and any other materials you may need so you won't be distracted by getting up to find things while you study.

If you're having a hard time retaining the information or organizing your notes, experiment with different methods. For example, try color-coding by subject with colored pens, highlighters, or post-it notes. If you learn better by hearing, try recording yourself reading your notes so you can listen while in the car, working out, or simply sitting at your desk. Ask a friend to quiz you from your flashcards, or try teaching someone the material to solidify it in your mind.

Step 4: Create Your Environment

It's important to avoid distractions while you study. This includes both the obvious distractions like visitors and the subtle distractions like an uncomfortable chair (or a too-comfortable couch that makes you want to fall asleep). Set up the best study environment possible: good lighting and a comfortable work area. If background music helps you focus, you may want to turn it on, but otherwise keep the room quiet. If you are using a computer to take notes, be sure you don't have any other windows open, especially applications like social media, games, or anything else that could distract you. Silence your phone and turn off notifications. Be sure to keep water close by so you stay hydrated while you study (but avoid unhealthy drinks and snacks).

Also, take into account the best time of day to study. Are you freshest first thing in the morning? Try to set aside some time then to work through the material. Is your mind clearer in the afternoon or evening? Schedule your study session then. Another method is to study at the same time of day that you will take the test, so that your brain gets used to working on the material at that time and will be ready to focus at test time.

Step 5: Study!

Once you have done all the study preparation, it's time to settle into the actual studying. Sit down, take a few moments to settle your mind so you can focus, and begin to follow your study plan. Don't give in to distractions or let yourself procrastinate. This is your time to prepare so you'll be ready to fearlessly approach the test. Make the most of the time and stay focused.

Of course, you don't want to burn out. If you study too long you may find that you're not retaining the information very well. Take regular study breaks. For example, taking five minutes out of every hour to walk briskly, breathing deeply and swinging your arms, can help your mind stay fresh.

As you get to the end of each chapter or section, it's a good idea to do a quick review. Remind yourself of what you learned and work on any difficult parts. When you feel that you've mastered the material, move on to the next part. At the end of your study session, briefly skim through your notes again.

But while review is helpful, cramming last minute is NOT. If at all possible, work ahead so that you won't need to fit all your study into the last day. Cramming overloads your brain with more information than it can process and retain, and your tired mind may struggle to recall even previously learned information when it is overwhelmed with last-minute study. Also, the urgent nature of cramming and the stress placed on your brain contribute to anxiety. You'll be more likely to go to the test feeling unprepared and having trouble thinking clearly.

So don't cram, and don't stay up late before the test, even just to review your notes at a leisurely pace. Your brain needs rest more than it needs to go over the information again. In fact, plan to finish your studies by noon or early afternoon the day before the test. Give your brain the rest of the day to relax or focus on other things, and get a good night's sleep. Then you will be fresh for the test and better able to recall what you've studied.

Step 6: Take a Practice Test

Many courses offer sample tests, either online or in the study materials. This is an excellent resource to check whether you have mastered the material, as well as to prepare for the test format and environment.

Check the test format ahead of time: the number of questions, the type (multiple choice, free response, etc.), and the time limit. Then create a plan for working through them. For example, if you have 30 minutes to take a 60-question test, your limit is 30 seconds per question. Spend less time on the questions you know well so that you can take more time on the difficult ones.

If you have time to take several practice tests, take the first one open book, with no time limit. Work through the questions at your own pace and make sure you fully understand them. Gradually work up to taking a test under test conditions: sit at a desk with all study materials put away and set a timer. Pace yourself to make sure you finish the test with time to spare and go back to check your answers if you have time.

After each test, check your answers. On the questions you missed, be sure you understand why you missed them. Did you misread the question (tests can use tricky wording)? Did you forget the information? Or was it something you hadn't learned? Go back and study any shaky areas that the practice tests reveal.

Taking these tests not only helps with your grade, but also aids in combating test anxiety. If you're already used to the test conditions, you're less likely to worry about it, and working through tests until you're scoring well gives you a confidence boost. Go through the practice tests until you feel comfortable, and then you can go into the test knowing that you're ready for it.

Test Tips

On test day, you should be confident, knowing that you've prepared well and are ready to answer the questions. But aside from preparation, there are several test day strategies you can employ to maximize your performance.

First, as stated before, get a good night's sleep the night before the test (and for several nights before that, if possible). Go into the test with a fresh, alert mind rather than staying up late to study.

Try not to change too much about your normal routine on the day of the test. It's important to eat a nutritious breakfast, but if you normally don't eat breakfast at all, consider eating just a protein bar. If you're a coffee drinker, go ahead and have your normal coffee. Just make sure you time it so that the caffeine doesn't wear off right in the middle of your test. Avoid sugary beverages, and drink enough water to stay hydrated but not so much that you need a restroom break 10 minutes into the test. If your test isn't first thing in the morning, consider going for a walk or doing a light workout before the test to get your blood flowing.

Allow yourself enough time to get ready, and leave for the test with plenty of time to spare so you won't have the anxiety of scrambling to arrive in time. Another reason to be early is to select a good seat. It's helpful to sit away from doors and windows, which can be distracting. Find a good seat, get out your supplies, and settle your mind before the test begins.

When the test begins, start by going over the instructions carefully, even if you already know what to expect. Make sure you avoid any careless mistakes by following the directions.

Then begin working through the questions, pacing yourself as you've practiced. If you're not sure on an answer, don't spend too much time on it, and don't let it shake your confidence. Either skip it and come back later, or eliminate as many wrong answers as possible and guess among the remaining ones. Don't dwell on these questions as you continue—put them out of your mind and focus on what lies ahead.

Be sure to read all of the answer choices, even if you're sure the first one is the right answer. Sometimes you'll find a better one if you keep reading. But don't second-guess yourself if you do immediately know the answer. Your gut instinct is usually right. Don't let test anxiety rob you of the information you know.

If you have time at the end of the test (and if the test format allows), go back and review your answers. Be cautious about changing any, since your first instinct tends to be correct, but make sure you didn't misread any of the questions or accidentally mark the wrong answer choice. Look over any you skipped and make an educated guess.

At the end, leave the test feeling confident. You've done your best, so don't waste time worrying about your performance or wishing you could change anything. Instead, celebrate the successful completion of this test. And finally, use this test to learn how to deal with anxiety even better next time.

Review Video: Test Anxiety
Visit mometrix.com/academy and enter code: 100340

Important Qualification

Not all anxiety is created equal. If your test anxiety is causing major issues in your life beyond the classroom or testing center, or if you are experiencing troubling physical symptoms related to your anxiety, it may be a sign of a serious physiological or psychological condition. If this sounds like your situation, we strongly encourage you to seek professional help.

Online Resources

Due to our efforts to try to keep this book to a manageable length, we've created a link that will give you access to all of your online resources:

mometrix.com/resources719/toeflessentials

It's Your Moment, Let's Celebrate It!

Share your story @mometrixtestpreparation